A GUIDE TO

WUTHERING HEIGHTS

JANE EASTON

WITH TONY BUZAN

Hodder & Stoughton

Cover photograph ©: The Ronald Grant Archive
Mind Maps: Anne Jones
Illustrations: Karen Donnelly

Orders: please contact Bookpoint Ltd, 130 Milton Park, Abingdon, Oxon
OX14 4SB. Telephone: (44) 01235 400414, Fax: (44) 01235 400454. Lines
are open from 9.00–6.00, Monday to Saturday, with a 24 hour message
answering service. Email address: orders@bookpoint.co.uk

Long renowned as the authoritative source for self-guided learning – with
more than 30 million copies sold worldwide – the *Teach Yourself* series
includes over 200 titles in the fields of languages, craft, hobbies, business and
education.

British Library Cataloguing in Publication Data
A catalogue record for this title is available from The British Library

ISBN 0 340 69707 5

First published 1998
Impression number   10 9 8 7 6 5
Year   2005 2004   2003   2002   2001

The 'Teach Yourself' name and logo are registered trade marks of
Hodder & Stoughton Ltd.

Typeset by Transet Limited, Coventry, England.
Printed in Great Britain for Hodder & Stoughton Educational, a division
of Hodder Headline Ltd, 338 Euston Road, London NW1 3BH by
Cox & Wyman Ltd, Reading, Berkshire.

CONTENTS

HOW TO STUDY

There are five important things you must know about your brain and memory to revolutionise the way you study:

- ◆ how your memory ('recall') works *while* you are learning
- ◆ how your memory works *after* you have finished learning
- ◆ how to use Mind Maps – a special technique for helping you with all aspects of your studies
- ◆ how to increase your reading speed
- ◆ how to prepare for tests and exams.

Recall during learning
– THE NEED FOR BREAKS

When you are studying, your memory can concentrate, understand and remember well for between 20 and 45 minutes at a time. Then it needs a break. If you carry on for longer than this without a break your memory starts to break down. If you study for hours non-stop, you will remember only a small fraction of what you have been trying to learn, and you will have wasted hours of valuable time.

So, ideally, *study for less than an hour*, then take a five to ten minute break. During the break listen to music, go for a walk, do some exercise, or just daydream. (Daydreaming is a necessary brain-power booster – geniuses do it regularly.) During the break your brain will be sorting out what it has been learning, and you will go back to your books with the new information safely stored and organised in your memory banks. We recommend breaks at regular intervals as you work through the Literature Guides. Make sure you take them!

Recall after learning
– THE WAVES OF YOUR MEMORY

What do you think begins to happen to your memory straight after you have finished learning something? Does it immediately start forgetting? No! Your brain actually *increases* its power and carries on remembering. For a short time after your study session, your brain integrates the information, making a more complete picture of everything it has just learnt. Only then does the rapid decline in memory begin, and as much as 80 per cent of what you have learnt can be forgotten in a day.

However, if you catch the top of the wave of your memory, and briefly review (look back over) what you have been studying at the correct time, the memory is stamped in far more strongly, and stays at the crest of the wave for a much longer time. To maximise your brain's power to remember, take a few minutes and use a Mind Map to review what you have learnt at the end of a day. Then review it at the end of a week, again at the end of a month, and finally a week before your test or exam. That way you'll ride your memory wave all the way there – and beyond!

The Mind Map ®
– A PICTURE OF THE WAY YOU THINK

Do you like taking notes? More importantly, do you like having to go back over and learn them before tests or exams? Most students I know certainly do not! And how do you take your notes? Most people take notes on lined paper, using blue or black ink. The result, visually, is boring! And what does *your* brain do when it is bored? It turns off, tunes out, and goes to sleep! Add a dash of colour, rhythm, imagination, and the whole note-taking process becomes much more fun, uses more of your brain's abilities, and improves your recall and understanding.

A Mind Map mirrors the way your brain works. It can be used for note-taking from books or in class, for reviewing what you have just studied and for essay planning for coursework and in tests or exams. It uses all your memory's natural techniques to build up your rapidly growing 'memory muscle'.

You will find Mind Maps throughout this book. Study them, add some colour, personalise them, and then have a go at drawing your own – you'll remember them far better! Stick them in your files and on your walls for a quick-and-easy review of the topic.

HOW TO DRAW A MIND MAP

1 Start in the middle of the page. This gives your brain the maximum room for its thoughts.
2 Always start by drawing a small picture or symbol. Why? Because a picture is worth a thousand words to your brain. And try to use at least three colours, as colour helps your memory even more.
3 Let your thoughts flow, and write or draw your ideas on coloured branching lines connected to your central image. These key symbols and words are the headings for your topic. Start like the Mind Map on page 17.
4 Then add facts and ideas by drawing more, smaller, branches on to the appropriate main branches, just like a tree.
5 Always print your word clearly on its line. Use only one word per line.
6 To link ideas and thoughts on different branches, use arrows, colours, underlining, and boxes (see page 13).

HOW TO READ A MIND MAP

1 Begin in the centre, the focus of your topic.
2 The words/images attached to the centre are like chapter headings: read them next.
3 Always read out from the centre, in every direction (even on the left-hand side, where you will have to read from right to left, instead of the usual left to right).

USING MIND MAPS

Mind Maps are a versatile tool – use them for taking notes in class or from books, for solving problems, for brainstorming with friends, and for reviewing and working for tests or exams – their uses are endless! You will find them invaluable for planning essays for coursework and exams. Number your main branches in the order in which you want to use them and off you go – the main headings for your essay are done and all your ideas are logically organised!

Super speed reading

It seems incredible, but it's been proved – the faster you read, the more you understand and remember! So here are some tips to help you to practise reading faster – you'll cover the ground more quickly, remember more, and have more time left for both work and play.

◆ First read the whole text (whether it's a lengthy book or an exam or test paper) very quickly, to give your brain an overall idea of what's ahead and get it working. (It's like sending out a scout to look at the territory you have to cover – it's much easier when you know what to expect!) Then read the text again for more detailed information.
◆ Have the text a reasonable distance away from your eyes. In this way your eye/brain system will be able to see more at a glance, and will naturally begin to read faster.
◆ Take in groups of words at a time. Rather than reading 'slowly and carefully' read faster, more enthusiastically.
◆ Take in phrases rather than single words while you read.
◆ Use a guide. Your eyes are designed to follow movement, so a thin pencil underneath the lines you are reading, moved smoothly along, will 'pull' your eyes to faster speeds.

Preparing for tests and exams

◆ Review your work systematically. Cram at the start of your course, not the end, and avoid 'exam panic'!
◆ Use Mind Maps throughout your course, and build a Master Mind Map for each subject – a giant Mind Map that summarises everything you know about the subject.
◆ Use memory techniques such as mnemonics (verses or systems for remembering things like dates and events).
◆ Get together with one or two friends to study, compare Mind Maps, and discuss topics.

AND FINALLY...

Have *fun* while you learn – it has been shown that students who make their studies enjoyable understand and remember everything better and get the highest grades. I wish you and your brain every success! (Tony Buzan)

HOW TO USE THIS GUIDE

This guide assumes that you have already read *Wuthering Heights*, although you could read 'Background' and 'The story of *Wuthering Heights*' before the novel. It is best to use the guide alongside the text. You could read the 'Who's who?' and 'Themes' sections without referring to the novel, but you will get more out of these sections if you do refer to it to check the points made in these sections, and especially when thinking about the questions designed to test your recall and help you think about the novel.

The 'Commentary' section can be used in a number of ways. One way is to read a chapter or part of a chapter in the novel, and then read the commentary for that section. Keep on until you come to a test section, test yourself – then have a break! Alternatively, read the commentary for a chapter or part of a chapter, then read that section in the novel, then go back to the commentary. Find out what works best for you.

'Topics for discussion and brainstorming' gives topics that could well feature in exams or provide the basis for coursework. It would be particularly useful for you to discuss them with friends, or brainstorm them using Mind Map techniques (see p. v).

'How to get an "A" in English Literature' gives valuable advice on what to look for in a text, and what skills you need to develop in order to achieve your personal best.

'The exam essay' is a useful 'night before' reminder of how to tackle exam questions, and 'Model answer' gives an example of an A-grade essay and the Mind Map and plan used to write it.

The questions

Whenever you come across a question in the guide with a star ✪ in front of it, think about it for a moment. You could even jot down a few words in rough to focus your mind. There is not usually a 'right' answer to these questions: it is important for you to develop your own opinions if you want to get an 'A'. The 'Test yourself' sections are designed to take you about 10–20 minutes each – which will be time well spent. Take a short break after each one.

Page numbers

Page numbers refer to the Penguin Classic edition, edited by David Daiches or the Penguin Popular Classic edition. If you have another edition, the page numbers may be slightly different, although the chapters will be the same.

EY TO ICONS

Themes and imagery

A **theme** is an idea explored by an author. **Imagery** refers to
the kind of word picture used to make the idea come alive.
Particular sorts of image are usually associated with each
theme. Whenever a theme is dealt with in the guide, the
appropriate icon is used. This means you can find where a
theme is just by flicking through the book. Go on – try it now!

Love		Death and sleep	
Imprisonment and freedom		Social class	
Nature		Books	
Outsiders		Religion	
Childhood		The supernatural	

 STYLE AND LANGUAGE

This heading and icon are used in the Commentary wherever
there is a special section on the author's choice of words and
imagery.

ACKGROUND

This chapter is about the historical and social context in which Brontë wrote *Wuthering Heights*. It is important for you to have an understanding of these things, but you must always relate your knowledge of the history to the novel itself.

Family background

Emily Brontë was born in 1818. Her father, Patrick Brontë became the clergyman at Haworth parsonage in Yorkshire, where Emily lived for most of her life. There were five sisters and one brother. Their mother died when Emily was very small, and two sisters died four years later. The surviving children, Charlotte, Branwell, Emily and Anne, were brought up by their aunt. They lived a very isolated life as children, and educated themselves by reading widely. The children had vivid imaginations and invented fantasy kingdoms called Angria and Gondal, writing many stories and poems about these places.

Emily spent a short time as a governess and later travelled to Brussels to study languages with her older sister, Charlotte. She returned to Haworth in 1842 and remained there until her death. A collection of her poems was published in 1846 and *Wuthering Heights* was published in 1847. She died of disease (probably tuberculosis) in 1848, aged only 29.

Her brother Branwell was a frustrated painter and writer who turned to drink and drugs and eventually died at 31 years of age. Anne became well known through her novels *Agnes Grey* and *The Tenant of Wildfell Hall*. Charlotte, the oldest sister became a successful novelist. *Jane Eyre* and *Villette* are two of her most famous works and these, like Emily's *Wuthering Heights*, are still widely read today.

Historical background

The Brontë children grew up as the Industrial Revolution was changing the face of England, Wales and Scotland. At the beginning of the 19th century, most people still lived and worked in the countryside, but some small towns were growing rapidly. As the century passed, hundreds of thousands of people moved to find work in huge new cities like Birmingham and Manchester. New factories, shipyards and railways created enormous wealth for a small group of manufacturers and business people. However, conditions for factory and mine workers were terrible. Even young children worked 12 and 14 hours a day, and families were torn apart by the long hours everyone had to work in order to survive. There was huge social unrest.

Although the Brontës lived in a quiet country area, they were not far from big new industrial towns like Halifax and Bradford. Their everyday lives might not have been touched directly by the Industrial Revolution and social changes in Britain, but they would have known about them from the magazines and newspapers that they read.

The characters in *Wuthering Heights* live lives that have been the same for generations, but there is a hint that things will not stay the same for ever. Heathcliff is the intruder, the one who does not fit in, because he is neither a servant nor a farm worker, nor a rich man's son. We never find out how he made his money during his three-year absence, but it is possible that he was an entrepeneur; a self-made businessman. Later in the novel, he becomes even richer by taking away the inheritances of Hareton and Linton. So even though he was not originally part of the correct social class, he becomes part of it later because he is wealthy.

Literary background

The rise of a new middle class meant that many more people could read, and the demand for exciting new forms of writing kept on growing. Printing technology made books and magazines much cheaper. Long novels were very popular and they were published in three parts – like a television serial. Another very popular way to publish novels was in shorter episodes in magazines. Magazine serials ran much longer, and were rather like modern television soaps, because they tended to end on a cliffhanger to make readers buy the next magazine!

There was still great prejudice towards women in 19th-century society, and it was unheard of for women to write plays, never mind more serious works. However, the success of Jane Austen and other female novelists such as Fanny Burney and Maria Edgeworth made serious writing more 'respectable'. It meant that the Brontë sisters stood a chance of having their novels published, although they took the precaution of writing under male pen-names at first. *Wuthering Heights* was published under the name of Ellis Bell, until the real author was discovered to be Emily Brontë. Many critics were shocked that a woman could write about scenes of violence and great feeling, and Emily received some unpleasant criticism, (as did the novels of Charlotte and Anne). However, as the century continued, *Wuthering Heights* came to be regarded as an important work of art.

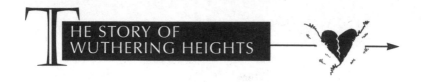

It is 1801. **Lockwood** is the first narrator of the novel. He is a rich young man who has left London to forget a love affair that went wrong. He moves to **Thrushcross Grange** in Yorkshire. Shortly afterwards he meets his surly and rather mysterious landlord, **Heathcliff**, who lives at **Wuthering Heights**, an old farmhouse on the moors. Heathcliff lives with a rough-mannered, handsome young man, a grumpy old servant named **Joseph** and a beautiful but sullen young woman. Lockwood is forced to stay overnight at the Heights and experiences strange dreams. The last dream is about the ghost of a girl named **Catherine**.

On Lockwood's return to the Grange, the housekeeper, **Nelly Dean**, begins to tell him the story. In 1771, old Mr **Earnshaw** returns from a business trip in Liverpool with a gypsy-like orphan boy named **Heathcliff**. No one knows anything about the child's origins, but Earnshaw's oldest child, **Hindley**, takes an instant dislike to Heathcliff. However, Earnshaw's daughter **Catherine**, forms a strong bond with Heathcliff, and they roam the **moors** together as children.

When **Earnshaw** dies, **Hindley** treats Heathcliff badly and tries to separate him from **Catherine**. One night, Catherine and Heathcliff wander to **Thrushcross Grange**, where they watch the spoilt **Edgar** and **Isabella Linton** through the window. **Catherine** is rescued from the dogs by the **Lintons** and cared for, but **Heathcliff** is sent home.

Catherine likes her new life as a young lady, but **Heathcliff** is going down in the world, thanks to Hindley's cruel treatment. Catherine sees more of **Edgar** and is attracted by his good **manners** and wealth. **Catherine** accepts Edgar's proposal of marriage, but also declares her passionate love for **Heathcliff**. However, Heathcliff leaves without hearing this, and disappears for **three** years.

Hindley turns to **drink** after his wife, Frances, **dies**. Only **Nelly** cares for his little son, **Hareton**. Mr and Mrs **Linton** die. Edgar and Catherine **marry** and **Nelly** moves to **Thrushcross Grange** to care for the young couple. **Hareton** is now alone with his father, whose drunkenness is worse than ever. **Heathcliff** returns six months after Catherine's marriage and moves into **Wuthering Heights** with **Hindley**, young **Hareton** and the servant, **Joseph**.

Heathcliff now begins to take revenge on **Hindley**, getting him to **gamble** his money away. He works on degrading **Hareton**, by stopping his **education** and ruining his character. **Heathcliff** causes trouble between Edgar and **Catherine**, who becomes very ill after a terrible argument. She **dies** after giving **birth** to her **daughter**, named **Cathy**. In the meantime, **Heathcliff** has eloped with **Isabella**, as part of his revenge on the **Linton** family. He treats her with great **cruelty**. After seeing a vicious **fight** between Heathcliff and **Hindley**, she runs away to **London**, where she bears **Linton Heathcliff**, their son.

Heathcliff is beside himself with **grief** after **Catherine's** death, but continues his brutal behaviour. He now has **Hindley** and **Hareton** in his power. **Hindley** dies in suspicious circumstances, leaving all his **property** and **land** mortgaged to Heathcliff in the form of **gambling** debts. Heathcliff now owns **Wuthering Heights**.

After **Isabella's** death, her son, **Linton**, is returned to **Heathcliff**. Linton is a miserable, **unhealthy** boy and Heathcliff **mistreats** him. Young **Cathy**, now sixteen, forms a relationship with **Linton**, but Heathcliff traps her and forces the young couple into **marriage**, so he can **inherit** Isabella's property. **Edgar Linton** dies and **Cathy** is left penniless. **Linton** dies soon afterwards. Heathcliff now owns all the property and lands of the **Linton** and **Earnshaw** families. He also **controls** the lives of **Hareton** and Cathy but his **bitterness** begins to wear out and he grows **obsessed** with the idea of being united with his **Catherine** once more. He **dies**, leaving Hareton and young Cathy to find **happiness** and the chance of a new **beginning** for themselves and their **descendants**.

HOW MUCH CAN YOU REMEMBER?

Try to fill in the missing words from this summary without looking back at the original. Feel free to use your own words if they have the same meaning.

It is 1801. _____ is the first narrator of the novel. He is a rich young man who has left London to try to forget a love affair that went wrong. He moves to _____ in Yorkshire. Shortly afterwards, he meets his surly and rather mysterious landlord, _____ who lives at _____ , an old farmhouse on the moors. Heathcliff lives with a rough-mannered, handsome young man, a grumpy old servant named _____ , and a beautiful but sullen young woman. Lockwood is forced to stay overnight at the Heights and experiences strange dreams. The last dream is about the ghost of a girl named _____ .

On Lockwood's return to the Grange, the housekeeper, _____ , begins to tell him the story. In 1771, old Mr _____ returns from a business trip in Liverpool with a gypsy-like orphan boy named _____ . No one knows anything about the child's origins, but Earnshaw's oldest child _____ , takes an instant dislike to Heathcliff. However, Earnshaw's daughter _____ , forms a strong bond with Heathcliff, and they roam the _____ together as children.

When _____ dies, _____ treats Heathcliff badly and tries to separate him from _____ . One night, Catherine and Heathcliff wander to _____ , where they watch the spoilt _____ and _____ through the window. _____ is rescued from the dogs by the _____ and cared for, but _____ is sent home.

_____ likes her new life as a young lady, but _____ is going down in the world, thanks to Hindley's cruel treatment. Catherine sees more of _____ and is attracted by his good _____ and wealth. _____ accepts Edgar's proposal of marriage, but also declares her passionate love for _____ . However, Heathcliff leaves without hearing this, and disappears for _____ years.

_____ turns to _____ after his wife, Frances, _____ . Only _____ cares for his little son. Mr and

Mrs _____ die. Edgar and Catherine _____ and
_____ moves to _____ to care for the young couple.
_____ is now alone with his father, whose drunkenness is
worse than ever. _____ returns six months after
Catherine's marriage and moves into _____ with
_____ , young _____ and the servant, _____ .

Heathcliff now begins to take revenge on _____ , getting
him to _____ his money away. He works on degrading
_____ , by stopping his _____ and ruining his
character. _____ causes trouble between Edgar and
_____ , who becomes very ill after a terrible argument. She
_____ after giving _____ to her _____ , named
_____ . In the meantime, _____ has eloped with
_____ , as part of his revenge on the _____ family.
He treats her with great _____ . After seeing a vicious
_____ between Heathcliff and _____ , she runs away
to _____ , where she bears _____ , their son.

Heathcliff is beside himself with _____ after _____
death, but continues his brutal behaviour. He now has
_____ and _____ in his power. _____ dies in
suspicious circumstances, leaving all his _____ and
_____ mortgaged to Heathcliff in the form of _____
debts. Heathcliff now owns _____ .

After _____ death, her son, _____ is returned to
_____ . Linton is a miserable, _____ boy and
Heathcliff _____ him. Young _____ , now sixteen,
forms a relationship with _____ , but Heathcliff traps her
and forces the young couple into _____ , so he can
_____ Isabella's property. _____ dies and
_____ is left penniless. _____ dies soon afterwards.
Heathcliff now owns all the property and lands of the
_____ and _____ families. He also _____ the
lives of _____ and Cathy, but his _____ begins to
wear out and he grows _____ with the idea of being
united with his _____ once more. He _____ ,
leaving Hareton and young Cathy to find _____ and the
chance of a new _____ for themselves and their
_____ .

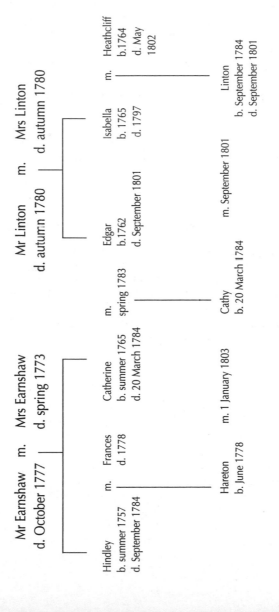

FAMILY TREE

Mr Earnshaw **m.** Mrs Earnshaw
d. October 1777   d. spring 1773

Mr Linton **m.** Mrs Linton
d. autumn 1780   d. autumn 1780

Hindley
b. summer 1757
d. September 1784

m. Frances
d. 1778

Catherine
b. summer 1765
d. 20 March 1784

m.
spring 1783

Edgar
b.1762
d. September 1801

m. September 1801

Isabella
b. 1765
d. 1797

m. Heathcliff
b.1764
d. May
1802

Hareton
b. June 1778

m. 1 January 1803

Cathy
b. 20 March 1784

Linton
b. September 1784
d. September 1801

The old generation

MR EARNSHAW

Earnshaw is Catherine and Hindley's father. Nelly says he has a *kind heart*. He means well by adopting Heathcliff, but does not reassure his own children. He has no patience with Hindley's jealousy and does not understand Catherine's high spirits.

JOSEPH

Joseph is a servant at Wuthering Heights. He thinks of himself as a religious person but is bad tempered and dislikes most people, particularly women. Nelly says he is the *wearisomest, self-righteous pharisee* (religious hypocrite) *that ever ransacked a Bible*. He often stirs up trouble between family members.

The next generation

HEATHCLIFF

Heathcliff is the adopted son of Mr Earnshaw. He is described as a *cuckoo* because he gradually takes away the inheritances of the Earnshaws and Lintons. Heathcliff is described throughout the novel as *the devil*, and other similar expressions. He is regarded with suspicion by the local people because of his dark, gypsy-like appearance. He loves Catherine Earnshaw passionately but Catherine will not marry out of her social class. Heathcliff runs away, returning to take revenge on Hindley and the Lintons. He becomes obsessed with Catherine after her death. (See page 11 for a Mind Map of his character.)

CATHERINE EARNSHAW

Catherine Earnshaw is a powerful character, who continues to influence or 'haunt' others after her death. As a child, she is mischievous and independent. Nelly describes her as a *wild wick* (lively) *slip ... but she had the bonniest eye and sweetest smile. I believe she meant no harm*. Catherine lives

11

by instinct and emotion, not by the usual common-sense rules of life. She is capable of deep love, but can be hurtful to others and finds it difficult to understand people who do not feel as passionately as herself. Her decision to marry Edgar places her in an impossible situation, and the strain of it eventually kills her. (See page 13 for a Mind Map of her character.)

HINDLEY EARNSHAW

Hindley is 14 years old at the beginning of Nelly's tale. He feels rejected by his father's love for Heathcliff, especially after being sent away to school. He later stops Heathcliff's education to prevent him from becoming a gentleman and is cruel and neglectful to Catherine. Frances's death tips him into despair. His drunkenness and violence bring a bad reputation to Wuthering Heights. Hindley ends up penniless and in debt to Heathcliff. His neglect of young Hareton acts as a strong contrast to the way Edgar brings up Cathy.

EDGAR LINTON

Edgar is first introduced to us by Heathcliff, who describes the boy as weak and pampered. Nelly calls Edgar a *soft thing* because he cannot stand up to Catherine's temper. He does not really understand Catherine and the couple are complete opposites. He tries to live by a moral code, but Catherine and Heathcliff are beyond this. Edgar is a complex character. He can be weak and unkind, as when he rejects his sister Isabella. However, he shows loyalty and devotion by shaking off depression after Catherine's death and being a good father to young Cathy.

ISABELLA LINTON

Isabella is described as *infantile*. She is no match for Catherine or Heathcliff because she has been so protected from life. Heathcliff uses her to get his hands on the Linton fortune. She falls in love with a romantic dream, not the real Heathcliff, although there are hints that she gets a strange enjoyment from his violent ways. However, she shows some spirit when she runs away to find a new life.

NELLY DEAN

Nelly Dean (Ellen) is the main narrator of the novel, and it is through her that we see most of the action. She is a hard working, honest and loyal woman who is not afraid to give her opinion. She shows great common sense, but even she sometimes misjudges situations, as when she ignores Catherine's illness in Chapter 11.

Nelly is well educated for her time, but has wisdom and common sense, not just book learning. Many characters confide in her, showing that she is regarded as trustworthy. She is brave, but sometimes it seems as if she is too used to violence, because she often describes terrible scenes in a very matter-of-fact way. We see her contentment at the end of the novel, as the marriage of her two beloved *nurslings* grows nearer, and happiness returns to Wuthering Heights.

The new generation

CATHY LINTON

Cathy is the daughter of Catherine and Edgar. When Lockwood first meets her, she seems to resemble the worst side of her mother. *She flung the tea back ... and resumed her chair in a pet ... her red underlip pushed out, like a child's, ready to cry.* This description shows Heathcliff's power to change even the most loving nature. Later, Nelly shows us the real Cathy, whose heart is sensitive and lively, and whose love is never fierce but deep and tender. Cathy can be cruel and thoughtless, as when she mocks Hareton's efforts to read, yet she is truly shocked by hearing about Heathcliff's wicked deeds. She is very loyal to Linton, despite his ungrateful behaviour and her loving nature helps to mend the quarrel between herself and Hareton. This is the beginning of hope for the new generation. (See page 15 for a Mind Map of her character.)

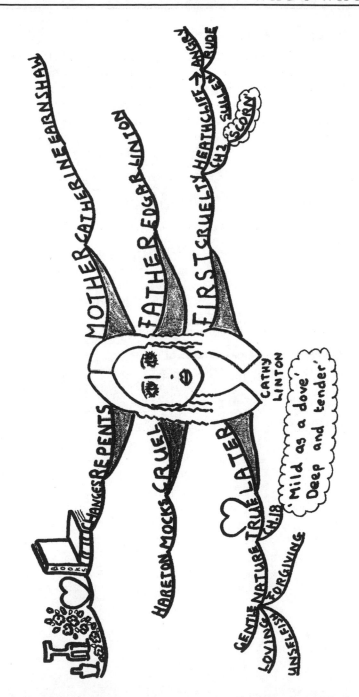

MOTHER CATHERINE EARNSHAW

FATHER EDGAR LINTON

FIRST CRUELTY HEATHCLIFF → ANGRY (H.2 SULLEN RUDE SCORN)

CATHY LINTON

CHANGES REPENTS

HARETON MOCKS CRUEL

GENTLE NATURE TRUE LATER (H.18)

LOVING FORGIVING

UNSELFISH

'Mild as a dove' Deep and tender'

HARETON EARNSHAW

Hareton is Hindley's son and is hated by Heathcliff for this reason. Hareton becomes a terrible echo of Heathcliff's own degradation by Hindley. Like Heathcliff, he is handsome and intelligent, but is made into little more than an animal. He is illiterate and foul mouthed and is encouraged to think of anything fine as worthless and *soft*. Hareton's instinctive love of beauty makes him change. Books are a way to improve his life and bring him closer to Cathy. He even shows love and forgiveness towards Heathcliff, and it is these qualities that help to bring about the new beginning at Wuthering Heights.

LINTON HEATHCLIFF

The son of Isabella and Heathcliff, Linton is a weak, sickly boy with a vicious side to his nature. Only Cathy loves and cares for him. Nelly dislikes his selfishness. He is despised by his father, who uses him to get at Cathy's inheritance.

LOCKWOOD

Lockwood is the first narrator of the novel. He is not a good judge of character and finds making relationships difficult, particularly with women. He is a rather snobbish, lonely man who always seems to be watching the lives of others, never a part of things.

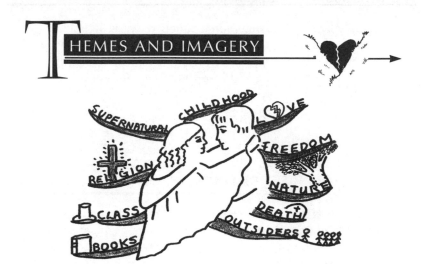

Themes

A theme is an idea developed or explored throughout a work (i.e a play, book, poem, etc.). The main themes of *Wuthering Heights* are shown on the Mini Mind Map above, and can be identified as follows:

- love
- imprisonment and freedom
- nature
- outsiders
- childhood
- death and sleep
- social class
- books
- religion
- the supernatural

Love

Romantic love is difficult for every character in the novel, even though Wuthering Heights is often thought of as a love story. Every relationship but one is broken by death or separation. Only Catherine and Hareton are given the chance of a happy, fruitful marriage.

Family love is also shown in a variety of ways. Relationships between family members are often marked by jealousy, cruelty or neglect. Even supposedly happy families like the Linton children seem spoiled and overprotected. Yet there are times when the family provides affection and love, such as in the relationship between Edgar Linton and his daughter Catherine. Nelly is also an important provider of family love, even though she is not related to any of the characters by blood.

Imprisonment and freedom

Throughout the novel, characters are often 'locked up', either physically or emotionally. This imprisonment might be caused by another person, such as when Heathcliff imprisons Isabella and Nelly, or it might be caused by the harsh weather, as when Lockwood cannot leave because of the snow. Edgar wants to protect young Catherine, so he stops her from going out of the grounds of Thrushcross Grange, but this is done from love, not greed or revenge.

Heathcliff and Catherine are free spirits as children. Even beatings cannot keep them imprisoned, and they often run away. Later on, Catherine is often described as sitting beside an open window. This is a sign of her need for freedom from responsibilities, even though she is grown up.

Nature

The changing seasons and weather have a strong effect on characters and events. *Wuthering Heights* was written almost 200 years ago, when there were no cars or televisions and country life was often very lonely. Bad weather could stop all contact with the outside world, and long dark winters were likely to cause gloom and depression.

Most importantly, nature is often described in connection with human emotions and activities in the novel. A good example of this is the night when Heathcliff leaves the Heights. The terrible storm which follows acts as an echo of the strong emotions felt by Catherine and Heathcliff. The freedom-loving young Heathcliff and Catherine are also associated with the descriptions of the untamed moors that they roam together.

Outsiders

The country people in the novel are often suspicious and unfriendly towards strangers. Heathcliff is the most important outsider in *Wuthering Heights*, and is treated with prejudice because he is dark skinned and looks like a gypsy. He is not a natural member of the Earnshaw family but is not a servant either, so people do not know how to place him.

Lockwood does not fit in because he is a rich Southerner and a stranger to the area. Heathcliff treats his own son, Linton, as if he were an outsider.

Childhood

The world of childhood is important to the novel. Children were treated with greater strictness than is usual nowadays. Although poorer children would have been working from an early age, richer children like Catherine and the Lintons were usually overprotected. However, many of the children in *Wuthering Heights* experience unusual levels of cruelty and neglect.

We meet almost all the major characters as children and read about them growing into adulthood. Emily Brontë has a great understanding about the way children think and behave. She writes about Hindley's treatment of the young Heathcliff and Catherine with sympathy. She is not sentimental about children, however, and understands that they can be cruel and jealous as well as funny and kind. For example, the description of young Hareton hanging puppies is shocking but believable, while Catherine dancing outside the door of the Heights creates an amusing picture of a lively, energetic girl.

Death and sleep

Death was much more common in the 19th century than nowadays. Women were more likely to die in childbirth, and many diseases were killers that are curable today. Emily Brontë knew this from personal experience after the deaths of her mother, two sisters and a brother.

There are many deaths in the novel. What is especially important is the way that the dead have such a powerful effect on the living. For example, Catherine's influence after death continues to affect others, especially Heathcliff. Even Lockwood, who knows nothing about her, is 'haunted' by her in a dream. When Mr Earnshaw dies, Heathcliff is no longer protected from Hindley's hatred, and Hindley destroys Heathcliff's life after Hindley loses his wife.

Sleep and death are often described in a very similar way. For instance, Lockwood gets in to the coffin-like closet bed and dreams about Catherine, a dead woman. Another example is Linton, who would rather stay in bed than go outside. This is a hint that he already believes himself to be close to the coffin and death.

Social class

It was difficult to move out of the class you were born into at the beginning of the 19th century. Nelly is unusual because she is well educated for a servant. Although servants were sometimes treated almost as family members, like Nelly and Joseph, they were still expected to know their place.

The way characters speak (**accent** and **dialect**) is used to show the difference in social class. Young Catherine cannot believe that Hareton is a relative of hers because he speaks like a farm worker. Level of education is also an important difference between the classes. Many of the poorer people would have been virtually illiterate, (unable to read or write). Hindley stops Heathcliff's education in order to prevent him from improving his chances in life.

Heathcliff is unusual because he is neither a servant nor has he inherited money like the Earnshaws and Lintons. He returns wealthy after a three-year absence, but no one knows how he has earned his money. He despises the pampered Lintons, who do not work for a living, but ironically he becomes a rich landowner himself after inheriting the Linton and Earnshaw properties.

Books

Books are mentioned frequently throughout the novel. People like Lockwood, the Lintons and Earnshaws would have had a lot of spare time, so reading was an important leisure activity.

Books are used in different ways. Lockwood uses them to escape reality and to relieve boredom, Joseph uses religious books to control the children whereas they unite Hareton and young Catherine.

One of the most important differences between the first Catherine and Edgar is described in terms of books. Catherine and Heathcliff represent strong emotion, whereas Edgar is part of the world of reason and controlled feelings. After a terrible argument between Catherine, Edgar and Heathcliff, Edgar goes to his library. Catherine cannot believe this: *What in the name of all that feels, has he to do with books when I am dying?*

Religion

Nearly everyone in the Brontës' time would have been a Christian, and most people went to church or chapel. The author herself was a parson's daughter. Yet there seems to be a criticism of religion in the novel. Most of this comes through Joseph, who is portrayed as a spiteful hypocrite. He uses Christianity to tell people that they are sinners going to hell, instead of concentrating on love and peace.

Wuthering Heights does not say much about God, which is unusual for a 19th century novel. Heathcliff and Catherine seem to worship nature more than God, which would have been shocking to many readers at that time.

The supernatural

Wuthering Heights contains a strong supernatural element. Catherine's ghost is described many times, and Heathcliff is believed to haunt the moors after his death. Local fairy stories and superstitions also come into it, as Joseph frequently refers to the two Catherines as *witches* who put spells on men. Nelly herself mentions local songs and stories about fairies.

21

Imagery

Imagery is language used to compare something and make us see it more vividly. For example, the first Catherine describes her love for Edgar Linton as *foliage in the woods* because it will eventually fade and die, like leaves on trees. She describes her love for Heathcliff as *the eternal rocks beneath*, because she believes her love for him is as necessary and everlasting as the ground we walk on.

Symbolism

Symbolism is the use of an object to represent something else. For example, a dove can mean peace, a rose may mean love. In *Wuthering Heights*, windows and doors are described as real objects, of course, but they are mentioned so many times that they stand for more than just parts of a house. Characters sometimes smash down doors as a way of getting at someone, or to escape from someone. Sometimes open windows symbolise a character's need for freedom.

Style

Style is the way an author writes, his or her individual 'signature'. For example, Emily Brontë uses many narrators, as well as moving the story backwards and forwards in time with the use of flashback. She uses imagery connected to nature, as mentioned earlier.

Another important feature of Brontë's style is her use of repetition. We often get confused about the characters because their names are identical or similar. Brontë does this to show how each generation is strongly influenced by the actions of the generation before them. Will they make the same mistakes? Will they be able to change the course of events or not?

Heathcliff and Catherine's relationship comes to nothing. Hareton and Cathy have similar names, but they succeed. The first generation do not make the right choices, whereas Cathy overcomes her false pride and Hareton improves himself. And Linton and Cathy's relationship is doomed, not just because Linton is so ill, but because he represents the worst

combination of the Linton family and Heathcliff. This is emphasised by the two parts of his name: Linton, for the weak, spoiled aspects of that family, and Heathcliff for the vicious and manipulative side. Cathy, on the other hand, inherits all the best qualities of her mother and father, and has a loving and supportive upbringing. Hareton has a similar upbringing to Heathcliff, but instead of being dragged down by bitterness and revenge, he makes a fresh start.

COMMENTARY

To make revision easier, the Commentary divides the novel into sections beginning with a brief preview which will prepare you for the section and help with last-minute revision. The Commentary comments on whatever is important in the section, focusing on the areas shown in the Mini Mind Map above.

ICONS

Wherever there is a focus on a particular theme, the icon for that theme appears in the margin (see p. xi for key). Look out, too, for the 'Style and language' sections. Being able to comment on style and language will help you to get an 'A' in your exam.

You will learn more from the Commentary if you use it alongside the novel itself. Read a section from the novel, then the corresponding Commentary section – or the other way around.

STARRED QUESTIONS

Remember that when a question appears in the Commentary with a star ✪ in front of it, you should stop and think about it for a moment. And **do remember to take a break** after completing each exercise!

Section 1 Chapters 1–3

CHAPTER 1
pages 45–50/19–23

◆ November 1801: Lockwood moves to Thrushcross Grange
◆ Meets Heathcliff, his landlord
◆ Lockwood unwelcome at Wuthering Heights

Lockwood is a rich young gentleman from the south of England who has moved to Thrushcross Grange, a mansion on the Yorkshire Moors. He describes the first meeting with his landlord Heathcliff at Wuthering Heights, Heathcliff's farmhouse. Although Heathcliff is rude and unwelcoming, Lockwood enters the farm. His thoughts take him back to the broken love affair which caused him to move to Yorkshire. ❂Why do you think he behaves like this towards the young woman whom he met on holiday? He then returns to the main story, at which point he is attacked by the dogs in the kitchen. Neither Heathcliff nor Joseph seem to care. Despite their treatment of him, Lockwood is determined to return the next day. ❂Why does he want to visit such unfriendly people again?

✎ STYLE AND LANGUAGE

'Wuthering' is a Yorkshire expression for stormy, rather like the strong emotions of the people who live there. Brontë also describes *stunted firs* and *gaunt thorns* near the farmhouse, which seem similar to the emotional state of the characters living there. Their lives are so bitter and unhappy, they are unable to 'grow'. The house itself is described like a fortress with its narrow windows and corners *defended* with large jutting stones. This suggests the suspicion of strangers which is shown to Lockwood.

 Lockwood is an outsider because he is a southerner and a visitor. He is frightened of romantic relationships and so stays apart from them. Heathcliff is also an outsider, but for different reasons. Brontë immediately introduces the contradictory side to Heathcliff's character by describing him as both a *gentleman* and a *gypsy*.

CHAPTER 2
pages 51–60/23–31

- ◆ November 1801, following day: Lockwood visits the Heights again
- ◆ He meets Hareton and Cathy
- ◆ Is trapped by snow, stays night

This chapter sets the scene for the tangle of relationships which is such a strong feature of the novel. Lockwood is confused by Heathcliff, Hareton and Cathy and so is the reader! As well as this, Lockwood's experiences of the area are of unfriendliness. He is not made welcome by the servants at Thrushcross Grange, so walks to Wuthering Heights in the freezing cold. Even the weather is hostile, and Joseph is unwilling to let him in. He gets his first glimpse of how brutal life is at the Heights in the way that Heathcliff responds to Cathy.

No one will help him to get home safely, and even worse, when he takes a lantern to guide himself, Joseph sets the dogs on him. Lockwood is shocked and hurt, so Heathcliff grudgingly allows him to stay the night.

Despite the strange behaviour of the people there, the kitchen inside is warm and cosy. Brontë often describes very ordinary, pleasant domestic surroundings, even though the characters may be in an emotional mess. This helps to make the novel more down to earth and believable.

Lockwood wants to escape the unpleasant atmosphere at the Heights, but the weather keeps him a prisoner.

Lockwood is puzzled by Hareton, who has rough manners and workman's hands, yet does not act like a servant. He cannot place him socially and manages to irritate the young man. ❶Why does Lockwood need to find out Hareton's identity and social class?

CHAPTER 3
pages 61–73/31–42

- ◆ Lockwood sleeps in closet bed
- ◆ Finds Catherine's diary (177–)

- Dreams about sermon, then Catherine
- Wakes up Heathcliff
- Walks back to Grange in snow

This is a very important chapter in the novel. Lockwood learns some facts about the family from Catherine's diary, which is another form of narrator.

Lockwood is hidden in the closet bed, and reads the diary, which is written in a religious book. He has two vivid dreams. The first is about a long sermon in a church, the second is a nightmare that Catherine's ghost is crying to be let in from the cold. He is so frightened in this dream that he tries to cut her wrist on the broken glass to stop her from coming through the window. His shouting wakes Heathcliff, who is first of all angry to find him there and then shocked to hear him mention Catherine. Lockwood and the reader get a glimpse of the strong emotions which rule Heathcliff, as he breaks down and begs the dead Catherine to return. The use of dreams and ghosts gives a sense of the overpowering, uncontrollable relationship once shared by the lovers.

There is further confusion when Lockwood gets lost in the snow on his way back home the following day.

The weather is harsh and changeable, rather like the emotions in this chapter. Lockwood is confused and frightened by his experiences at the Heights, just as he gets lost in the snow later. It is as if he cannot be sure of anything in this strange place.

Both Catherine's diary and Lockwood's dream about Jabes Branderham describe religion being used as a punishment. In addition, Catherine's diary is written in a religious book, which shows her lack of respect for conventional religion.

The closet bed is rather like a coffin, and the idea of death is emphasised by Lockwood dreaming of the dead Catherine.

Questions to ask yourself

? Why does Lockwood try to push Catherine away by hurting her in the dream?

? Does this remind you of his actions at another time? Look back to Chapter 1, p. 48/21, and compare the two events. What do they tell us about his relationships with women?

now, take a break, before reading about family jealousy, a religious bigot — and death

November 1801, Lockwood arrives at Thrushcross Grange, unwelcomed and confused by Heathcliff and strange household at Wuthering Heights. He dreams about a dead girl whom he has never met.

Section 2 Chapters 4–7

CHAPTER 4
pages 74–81/42–8

- Nelly begins her narration; we go back in time to about 1771
- Mr Earnshaw takes a trip to Liverpool, returns with Heathcliff
- Anger and jealousy amongst the children

The return of Mr Earnshaw from Liverpool with an orphan boy causes trouble in the family. Catherine and Hindley are upset because their father seems to have forgotten or broken their presents for the sake of the strange child. Heathcliff looks like a gypsy and does not speak English, and is described right from the start as an 'intruder'. He also seems *hardened* and *insensible* to kindness or cruelty, which introduces the reader to the bad side of his character. Nelly also dislikes him, although Catherine soon makes friends with the new boy. Hindley hates him, however. ❍What is Hindley so afraid of? What does he mean when he calls Heathliff a *beggarly interloper*?

We see the calculating side of Heathcliff when he blackmails Hindley by threatening to tell Mr Earnshaw of his beatings. Hindley does exchange his horse as Heathcliff orders, but still attacks Heathcliff. Nelly says that although she did not believe Heathcliff was vindictive, she later realised that she was completely wrong. This suggests that Heathcliff will get his revenge eventually. Brontë is setting the scene for what Heathcliff does later in the novel.

We are not given a picture of childhood happiness here. Instead, the children are violent and jealous, yet Heathcliff is cool and strangely without emotion for such a young boy.

Heathcliff is very much the outsider, sometimes described as *it* instead of 'he' and as an *interloper*. His lack of English and dark colouring also make the household prejudiced and suspicious of him. ❍Why does Nelly say that the history of his life is a *cuckoo's*?

CHAPTER 5
pages 82–5/48–51

◆ 1771–7: Mr Earnshaw becomes ill
◆ Hindley more badly behaved; he and father clash
◆ Hindley sent away to school
◆ Earnshaw dies, October 1777

Mr Earnshaw's health begins to fail. This is one of the many examples of illness and decay and death which are repeated throughout the novel. He and Hindley clash, not helped by Joseph's interfering ways. Catherine is misunderstood by her father also, which makes her more naughty, and hardens her. She is, however, extremely upset when Earnshaw dies in front of the fire one stormy October evening. Nelly later sees the two children comforting each other and wishes they could all be safe in heaven. ❍Why does Brontë describe a storm at the time of Earnshaw's death? What is this literary device called?

Mr Earnshaw's death makes Catherine and Hindley orphans. It also represents the end of Heathcliff's protection and security, although we do not know this yet.

Joseph uses his knowledge to influence Mr Earnshaw and turn him against the children. Once again, religion is used to punish, instead of helping.

Understanding Catherine

? Remind yourself of the description of Catherine on pp. 83–4/49. (*Certainly, she had ways with her ... beg to be forgiven*). Make a Mini Mind Map, using key words which describe her character. What do you think of her?

? Add to the Mind Map after you have read Chapter 8 and see if your opinion has changed.

next, family violence — and an adventure at Thrushcross Grange! But take a break first

CHAPTER 6

pages 86–92/51–6

- ◆ 1797: Hindley is now the master of the house; returns home with a wife, Frances
- ◆ Hindley begins Heathcliff's 'degradation'
- ◆ Heathcliff takes on role of narrator to Nelly, describing his and Catherine's adventures at Thrushcross Grange (pp. 88–92/53–6)
- ◆ Hindley orders Heathcliff to stay away from Catherine

This is another key chapter in the novel, as it sows the seeds for the divisions which grow between Catherine and Heathcliff. It also shows the beginning of Heathcliff's degradation by Hindley.

Nonetheless, Hindley's cruelty brings Catherine and Heathcliff closer together at first. He stops Heathcliff's education and makes him work as a farm labourer. Heathcliff and Catherine frequently run off to escape Joseph and Hindley, and Nelly describes the children as *unfriended creatures.*

One Sunday evening, the children are caught peering through the windows into Thrushcross Grange, home of the Linton family. They are so unwanted by their own family that they are amazed to see the beautiful, luxurious surroundings. But the spoiled young Edgar and Isabella are bad tempered in spite of being so well-cared for, and are quarrelling over a dog. Heathcliff despises the brother and sister right from the beginning, which prepares us for his behaviour later in the novel.

Heathcliff returns to tell the Earnshaws that Catherine is safe at the Grange. The following day, Mr Linton visits the Heights and lectures Hindley about the lack of guidance he is giving Catherine. Hindley warns Heathcliff to keep away from her.

Nelly does not realise it, but Frances suffers a fatal illness which will eventually kill her. Brontë emphasises the frequency of death by describing a dying woman at a funeral.

Hindley stops Heathcliff's education because he is deliberately trying to make sure that Heathcliff never becomes a 'gentleman'. Heathcliff also has to work outside like a farmhand, something which middle-class and upper-class people did not do.

The incident at the Grange further emphasises the class differences between Catherine and Heathcliff. Catherine is allowed to stay there and is treated like a princess. Heathcliff tells Nelly that Catherine *is a young lady and they made a distinction between her treatment and mine*. In fact, the Lintons assume that Heathcliff is a thief because of his dark colouring.

Over to you

?   Remind yourself of the descriptions of Edgar and Isabella in this chapter. Make a Mind Map, comparing them with Catherine.

?   Make a list of the reasons why Heathcliff is so scornful about the young Lintons.

now take a break. Afterwards, find out if scruffy Heathcliff has a chance with the new, elegant Catherine

CHAPTER 7
pages 93–103/56–65

◆ Christmas 1777: Catherine returns to Wuthering Heights as a young lady
◆ Heathcliff is more neglected and dirty
◆ Heathcliff attacks Edgar, swears revenge on Hindley
◆ Nelly's narration stops temporarily and she and Lockwood chat

Catherine returns. Not only is she beautifully dressed, but she behaves in a much more calm and polite way. ❁Why does Heathcliff behave so awkwardly towards her now?

The contrast between Heathcliff and her is painful. Hindley enjoys humiliating the boy. He treats him like one of the servants.

Despite this, Nelly encourages Heathcliff to clean himself and he promises to be good. He is jealous of Edgar Linton's blonde good looks and the wealth he will inherit, as he thinks these things will make Catherine prefer Edgar. Nelly cheers him up by telling him *a good heart will help you to a bonny face ... you're fit for a prince in disguise.* ❍Is Nelly correct? Could Heathcliff have won Catherine's affection by being nicer?

Heathcliff attacks Edgar and is banned from Christmas dinner. ❍Why do you think Catherine is angry at Edgar? Why does she defend Heathcliff?

Although she pretends to be happy, we see the loving side to Catherine, when she secretly weeps over Heathcliff's punishment. Nelly and Catherine comfort the beaten boy, who swears revenge on Hindley, despite Nelly's words of warning. Catherine and Heathcliff spend time together, and we get a sense of the strong bond between them.

The narration returns to the present, then Nelly moves the story to the summer of 1778.

Heathcliff is more left out of the family than before.

Lockwood is a well-educated man, but Nelly Dean is more realistic and has greater common sense than him. She has read widely, but also uses her experience of life to help her to understand people. Books do not always teach wisdom, certainly not in Lockwood's case.

If only ...

? A turning point for Heathcliff happens in this chapter. Where do you think it comes?

? Could it have been prevented, or does Heathcliff's character make this bound to happen?

? Write down your opinions in Mind Map form, using quotations from the chapter to prove what you say.

next, Hindley takes to the bottle, while Catherine can't make up her mind. Find out more — after the break

Heathcliff adopted by Mr Earnshaw. Hatred begins between Heathcliff and Hindley. Growing bond between Catherine and Heathcliff, but Catherine has changed into a lady.

Section 3 Chapters 8–12

CHAPTER 8

pages 104–13/65–73

- June 1778: Hareton Earnshaw born to Hindley and Frances
- Frances dies soon afterwards, Hindley turns to drink and gambling
- Wuthering Heights loses respectability
- Catherine now 15, friendship with Edgar and Heathcliff difficult
- Heathcliff's character worse
- Edgar experiences Catherine's temper for the first time

Frances dies and Hindley goes downhill fast. Brontë shows here how unstable and unpredictable life is for the characters at Wuthering Heights. We have already met Hareton, an uneducated and surly young man. At this point in the novel we see him as a motherless baby, unwanted by his unhappy and drunken father.

The novel describes scenes of increasing degradation and violence. This family is falling apart. Hindley's treatment of Heathcliff is *enough to make a fiend of a saint*, and indeed, Nelly describes Heathcliff as becoming *diabolical*, or like the devil. No one respectable visits the house any more, except for Edgar Linton, who is still friendly with Catherine.

Catherine has grown into a beautiful young woman, although she is *haughty and headstrong*. However, Catherine feels confused and full of conflict because Heathcliff and Edgar dislike each other so much. This is the beginning of the great problems in her life. ❊Why does Catherine like each man so much, even though they are complete opposites? Have you ever had problems because of friendships with two very different people?

Brontë shows us how difficult the situation is when Catherine and Heathcliff argue about the almanack, which is a type of calendar. He has been keeping a record of how much time she spends with Edgar. Catherine is cross and tells him *it's no company at all, when people know nothing and say nothing*. ❊What is she saying about Heathcliff now? Why has he changed so much? When Edgar arrives, Nelly notices a strong difference between the two young men. *The contrast resembled what you see in exchanging a bleak, hilly, coal country for a beautiful fertile valley.*

❊Who is described as the coal country and who is compared to a beautiful valley? What do we learn about Edgar's voice and accent straight after this quote? What do you think about the young men now?

Catherine loses her temper after the argument with Heathcliff. She is physically violent. Edgar is shocked by this side of her and tries to leave, but Catherine's tears bring him back. ❊Nelly uses a **simile** to describe Edgar's lack of willpower on p. 112/73 – can you find it? Why does she also say Edgar is *doomed*?

At the end of the chapter, Hindley returns home raving drunk, and Nelly takes the bullets from his gun to protect the household from his rage. This is yet another example of the emotional and physical violence in this chapter. Like death, Nelly describes it in rather a matter-of-fact way, and it is Edgar Linton, not a household member, who seems most shocked by Catherine's behaviour. Perhaps Nelly has become hardened because of the constant violence and cruelty at the Heights.

Frances dies, and this affects the whole household, because Hindley is so unhappy that he turns to drink and gambling. Nelly does not spend a lot of time describing the death, which adds to the feeling that it is almost a common event.

The three young people feel love for each other, but none of them seems improved or made happy by it. Heathcliff is sullen and jealous, Catherine is selfish and bad - tempered and Edgar is weak and under her spell.

Catherine grows up

? Look back at your notes about Catherine from Chapter 5 onwards. Write a few sentences to explain how she has changed.

a near miss, a mysterious disappearance and a marriage follow — but for now, take a break

CHAPTER 9
pages 114–29

- ◆ 1780: Hareton rescued from Hindley's violence by Heathcliff
- ◆ Heathcliff longs for Hindley's death
- ◆ Catherine asks Nelly's advice about Edgar's proposal of marriage
- ◆ She compares Heathcliff and Edgar
- ◆ Heathcliff overhears, but misunderstands the conversation - leaves the Heights

- Catherine falls into fever after looking for Heathcliff in storm
- Mr and Mrs Linton die from fever
- Catherine becomes more moody and bad tempered
- April 1783: Edgar and Catherine married, Nelly goes with them to Grange, leaving young Hareton behind
- Return to Lockwood's narration

This is another key chapter in the novel. It highlights the impossible situation Catherine is in, with regard to Edgar and Heathcliff. It also shows the strength of Heathcliff's feelings towards Hindley. *He expressed ... the intensest anguish at having made himself the instrument of thwarting his own revenge.* ❂What does Brontë mean by this? Why should Heathcliff want Hareton dead?

Catherine seems unsure about her decision to marry Edgar. She does not realise that Heathcliff is listening in the shadows. ❂Why doesn't Nelly warn her?

Catherine describes a dream, that she believes means *I've no more business to marry Edgar Linton than I have to be in heaven,* and says that such a marriage would never have crossed her mind if Hindley had not brought Heathcliff so *low.* As she is explaining that it would *degrade* her to marry Heathcliff now, he slips out, believing that she despises him. He misses the rest of her statement, where she declares her feelings for him.❂Why do you think Nelly keeps quiet? Do you agree with what she does?

Catherine will not accept that anything could come between them, even her marriage to Edgar. She says *Nelly, I am Heathcliff.* Nelly does not understand. She tells Catherine that either she does not understand how marriage changes one's life, or that she is a *wicked, unprincipled girl.* ❂Is it possible to break society's rules about love and marriage? Is Catherine selfish or naive or ... ? What do you think?

The morning after Heathcliff's disappearance, Nelly finds Catherine in the kitchen with the front door and windows open. ❂Can you explain how this fits in with the windows and doors symbolism in the novel?

We see the effect of the emotional pressure on Catherine, who becomes more irritable and quick tempered. She marries Edgar three years later and Nelly is forced to go with the young couple to the Grange, leaving little Hareton behind.

Once again, love is not straightforward. Catherine's love for Edgar is shallow, but she is not willing to risk her social position with Heathcliff. She loses her soul mate when he runs away. Catherine takes Nelly's affection for granted and is rude and ungrateful.

The storm is used as a symbol of the emotional tension between Catherine and Heathcliff. The fire is a symbol of the home, and when it is put out by the storm, this suggests that the home is threatened by the violence and quarrels of those who live there.

Torn between two lovers

? Make a chart to show the difference between the descriptions of Heathcliff and Edgar in Chapters 8–9. Find these on pp. 110, 122, 121 and 122/71, 73, 80, 81.
Some examples have been done for you.

Words used about Edgar | Words used about Heathcliff
foliage in the woods | eternal rocks beneath
moonbeam | lightning

? When you have completed the list, do the following tasks.
a) Write a sentence explaining what the words used to describe Edgar make you think about his character. Do the same for Heathcliff.
b) Write your own simile for each man to explain his character. For example, Edgar is like a gentle spring day, Heathcliff is like a blazing summer afternoon.

read on for more scandal. Twisted love and strife – after the break

CHAPTER *10*
pages 130–46/88–102

- ◆ Winter 1801:Lockwood ill
- ◆ Nelly returns to the story
- ◆ September 1783: Catherine and Edgar contented, but hints of Catherine's despair
- ◆ Heathcliff returns after three-year absence
- ◆ Catherine's joy, Edgar's jealousy, Nelly's anxiety
- ◆ Isabella falls for Heathcliff, Catherine tries to talk her out of it
- ◆ Hindley's behaviour worse under Heathcliff's influence

Edgar is surprised to see Heathcliff changed into a well-grown and intelligent-looking man with a dignified manner, instead of the *gypsy, the ploughboy* he remembered, but Nelly thinks she can still see the old wildness in Heathcliff's eyes. Catherine is so excited she does not notice Edgar's jealousy. Heathcliff still harbours violent feelings towards Hindley. They act as if Edgar is not there.

Later, Catherine describes how much despair and misery she felt when Heathcliff left – she had even rebelled against God in her anger. ❍Can you see a similarity in the way Catherine speaks about religion in her dream in Chapter 9?

An unexpected twist comes when the 18-year-old Isabella falls in love with Heathcliff. Edgar realises that although Heathcliff seems changed on the outside, his mind is unchangeable, and unchanged. ❍Remind yourself of the change in Catherine when she returned from the Grange in Chapter 7. Is there a similarity in the way Catherine and Heathcliff have changed?

Catherine warns Isabella about Heathcliff's real nature. ❍What does this tell us about Catherine's love for Heathcliff?

We begin to see that Heathcliff's revenge is taking shape, as Nelly mentions Hindley's increased drinking and gambling.

 STYLE AND LANGUAGE

The change that Heathcliff will bring to Edgar and Catherine's marriage is emphasised by the descriptions of him in shadow. This is a contrast to the autumn sunshine described by Nelly a few sentences before. Heathcliff also looks up to the windows, which reflect the moon but show no light inside. It is as if the house holds no welcome for him; he does not belong there.

Nelly uses a striking image to explain her fears. *I felt that God had forsaken the stray sheep there to its own wicked wanderings, and an evil beast prowled between it and the fold, waiting his time to spring and destroy.* ❂Who is the evil beast, who is the stray sheep?

Despite Heathcliff's transformation into a gentleman, he is still regarded with suspicion. More importantly, Edgar's worries about Isabella are partly because Heathcliff might be after his family's money. Women had no right to their own money once they were married, so Isabella might be Heathcliff's means of getting at the Linton fortune.

Isabella is young and naive. Her love is a strong contrast with Catherine and Heathcliff's love.

CHAPTER 11

pages 147–57/102–11

- ◆ 4 January 1784: Nelly wants to warn Hindley about Heathcliff
- ◆ Nelly meets young Hareton
- ◆ Heathcliff courts Isabella
- ◆ Catherine and Heathcliff quarrel
- ◆ Edgar steps in, violence between the two men
- ◆ Catherine and Edgar quarrel, she has a fit

Nelly visits the Heights, where she meets the foul-mouthed and violent young Hareton. She learns that Heathcliff has stopped the child's education and is encouraging his bad behaviour. ❂Why is Heathcliff doing this? Can you explain how this is an example of repetition in the novel?

The discovery of Isabella and Heathcliff kissing provokes a huge row. Catherine is shocked by Heathcliff's lust for revenge, and is also horrified when he calls her a *tyrant*. It is clear that he is still bitter about her treatment of him when they were younger.

The angry scene between Heathcliff, Edgar and Catherine which follows, highlights the differences between Edgar's world and the world of Catherine and Heathcliff. Catherine has no illusions about Heathcliff, but is disgusted by Edgar's weakness and emotional coldness. She and Heathcliff take sides, but the conflict triggers Catherine's mental illness. She is unable to cope with the contradictions in her life.

Catherine then falls into a fit, brought about by extreme emotion. Edgar wants her to choose between himself and Heathcliff. Nelly is unsympathetic about her mental state, believing Catherine is just being manipulative.

Catherine throws the door key into the fire because she thinks that Edgar should have the courage to stand up to Heathcliff or else let him go. This is another example of imprisonment.

Edgar is as worried by the idea of Heathcliff inheriting the family fortune as he is by the thought that Isabella might make an unhappy marriage.

Nelly's fears about Hindley's safety at the hands of Heathcliff trigger off some sort of vision. She thinks she sees Hindley as the young boy with whom she used to play.

Spot the difference

?   In Chapter 10, Heathcliff describes his hatred of Isabella's eyes. Compare that description with what he says about the vacant blue eyes of the Lintons.

?   Now look back at your chart on Heathcliff and Edgar and add details about the difference in their looks.

starvation and family breakdown ... where will it end? But first, take a break

CHAPTER 12
pages 158–70/111–22

- ◆ Isabella upset, Edgar escapes in books
- ◆ Catherine starves herself – Nelly does not take her seriously
- ◆ She becomes delirious – Edgar frightened, then angry with Nelly
- ◆ Catherine rejects Edgar, also Nelly
- ◆ Isabella's dog hanged by Heathcliff
- ◆ Later, Isabella vanishes – eloped with Heathcliff
- ◆ Edgar is finished with his sister

We see how strong the difference between the Lintons and Catherine is, in the ways they express their unhappiness. Edgar hides in the library, Isabella is quietly miserable, whereas Catherine becomes ill. ❂What do you think about Nelly's mistrust of Catherine's illness?

Catherine predicts her death. She also says that she is *past wanting* Edgar. This is a sign of how far she is unable to cope with the conflict in her life. Death is a way out of this.

The hanging of Isabella's dog is a symbol of Heathcliff's violent feelings towards her. This incident is especially shocking when we realise that Isabella is going to be married to him. ❂Why does Edgar reject his sister after she elopes with Heathcliff? Do you think he should have done anything else?

Edgar cannot cope with Catherine's extremes of emotion and he retreats to books so he does not have to face up to her anger. For him, his library is an escape from the problems in his relationship. It is another sign of the differences between them.

Catherine's demand for the window to be opened on a winter's day, is a sign of how trapped and misunderstood she feels. She also tells stories about the feathers she is tearing from her pillow because they remind her of the birds and moors of her childhood, another example of her need for freedom.

Hindley's behaviour goes downhill and he neglects Hareton. Catherine in conflict – Edgar or Heathcliff? Heathcliff leaves. When he returns, Catherine and Edgar are married. Catherine has a breakdown. Isabella elopes – Heathcliff's revenge is beginning to take shape.

Section 4 Chapters 13–17

CHAPTER 13

pages 171–82/122–31

- ◆ Catherine has a brain fever, is nursed by Edgar
- ◆ March 1784: she recovers, but continues to predict her own death; she is pregnant
- ◆ Edgar receives an apologetic note from Isabella, but does not reply
- ◆ 13 March 1784: Isabella and Heathcliff return to the Heights;
- ◆ Nelly receives a letter from Isabella
- ◆ Isabella now the narrator; she describes her terrible life with Heathcliff
- ◆ Life at the Heights with Hindley, Heathcliff, Hareton and Joseph

- Hindley still having violent urges when he is drunk – warns Isabella
- Isabella's first night at the Heights; Joseph unkind and unwelcoming
- Heathcliff's harsh treatment of Isabella – she hates him

Isabella's letter to Nelly gives us another character's viewpoint on how low life has sunk at the Heights. Her descriptions of the violence and misery there form a strong contrast with the happy memories Catherine has of her old home. ❂How many examples can you find of the bad conditions and behaviour there?

The reader gets an idea of how badly Heathcliff is acting by Isabella's use of **rhetorical questions**. *Is he mad ... is he a devil?* She also asks Nelly *what*, not 'who', she has married, which is similar to the way Heathcliff is called *it* earlier in the novel.

Joseph seems to feed on the unhappiness at the house, given his cruel pleasure in Isabella's misery. Despite the difference in accent and social class he has more control over the house than she does. Heathcliff blames Edgar for Catherine's illness and threatens to take revenge by punishing Isabella.

STYLE AND LANGUAGE

Heathcliff is compared to an animal once more when Isabella says *a tiger or a venomous serpent could not rouse terror in me equal to that which he wakens.*

Another example of style is the state of the house, which is like a reflection of the lives of the people who live there. Heathcliff's bedroom shows signs of violence, with everything torn and broken.

Joseph locks the gate *as if he lived in an ancient castle*, while Hindley warns Isabella to lock her door, to protect herself from his drunken rages. The inhabitants are also imprisoned in their emotions.

The crocuses are a sign of spring and new life, and Catherine is pleased to see them when she comes out of her fever, because they remind her of the Heights. Nonetheless, she knows she will never see them, or the moors again.

What is happening to Isabella?

? Has your opinion about Isabella's character changed in any way?

? In what way do you think she is being influenced by the atmosphere at Wuthering Heights?

find out more about Isabella's marriage from hell – after the break

CHAPTER 14
pages 183-91/132-9

- ◆ March 1784: Edgar is still unforgiving of Isabella
- ◆ Nelly visits the Heights, is shocked by the state of the place
- ◆ Isabella being dragged down to its level – only Heathcliff looks good
- ◆ Nelly lectures Isabella about her foolishness; Heathcliff insists on seeing Catherine
- ◆ He compares the depth of his love for Catherine with Edgar's
- ◆ Heathcliff describes Isabella's love for him – suggests that she enjoys cruelty
- ◆ He threatens to imprison Nelly if she stops him from seeing Catherine
- ◆ Nelly promises to take Catherine a letter from him
- ◆ The narration returns to Lockwood, who thinks about his attraction to Cathy and worries that she may have turned out like her mother

In this chapter, Nelly reports on the state of the Heights and its inhabitants. Heathcliff seems to infect everyone there with his hatred and brutality. Isabella is so paralysed with the atmosphere that she cannot even keep herself clean. We also see the moralistic side of Nelly when she blames Isabella for her predicament. Yet Nelly is shocked by Heathcliff's sadistic behaviour towards his wife. What is strange is that Isabella seems to come to life. It seems as if she can feel emotion only when he is acting badly towards her.

The chapter is also important in the way it lets us see Heathcliff's moral code. He despises Edgar's morality with its ordinary *duty* and *humanity*. He believes Catherine and himself are above such petty, everyday rules. We also see Heathcliff's obsessive desire for revenge when he exclaims *the more the worms writhe, the more I yearn to crush out their entrails.*

Nelly is torn between loyalty to Edgar and fear of what Heathcliff might do, so agrees to take a letter.

The narration returns to Lockwood, who mentions his attraction to Cathy. There is a feeling of history repeating itself when he speaks of her *brilliant eyes*, and worries that she might turn out like her mother.

STYLE AND LANGUAGE

Brontë uses a series of vivid similes and **metaphors** to describe the nature of Heathcliff's love for Catherine. *Catherine has a heart as deep as I have; the sea could be as readily contained in that horse-trough, as her whole affection be monopolized by him.* He uses 'horse-trough' to pour scorn on Edgar's earthly, limited love. It acts as a contrast with the power and magnificence of the sea, which is like the love Heathcliff and Catherine share. He believes that Catherine is *in hell* being surrounded by people who cannot feel like herself and Heathcliff. They *might as well plant an oak in a flower pot, and expect it to thrive.* This metaphor contrasts Catherine's untamed, passionate nature with Edgar's calmer, more domestic love.

Isabella is forced upstairs by Heathcliff. Nelly is threatened with imprisonment at the Heights if she does not take a letter to Catherine. This is an earlier version of what happens to Cathy and herself later in the novel.

The mystery of Heathcliff

? Heathcliff's behaviour goes from bad to worse. Add examples of his actions to your Heathcliff Mini Mind Map. Remember to use keyword quotations and page references.

Heathcliff and Catherine have a passionate meeting — find out more after your break

CHAPTER 15
pages 192–200/139–46

- January 1802: Lockwood's narration opens the chapter
- Nelly takes up the story; 19 March 1784 - Catherine still very weak
- She reads letter, then Heathcliff enters and realises she is dying
- Emotional scene between them; Catherine faints
- Edgar returns, tries to bring Catherine round, but she is in a deep faint
- Heathcliff will not leave the garden, so he can be near her

Another important chapter, in which Heathcliff's passionate speech shows the terrible result of Catherine's decision to marry Edgar (pp. 197–8/143–4). Once full of life and energy, Catherine now seems almost ghost-like in her white gown and pale, haggard face. Her manner is dreamy, her gaze *out of this world*. All these descriptions emphasise that she is near death. Only Heathcliff has the power to temporarily lift her from this state. We see the strength of their passion, physical as well as emotional, as she pulls out a lock of Heathcliff's hair during their embrace, while he leaves bruises on her arm from holding her too tightly.

In his agony Heathcliff accuses her of betraying her own heart. Brontë seems to be suggesting that Catherine is dying because she went against her natural instincts by marrying Edgar. ❂Do you agree with this point of view? Could Catherine and Heathcliff have had a happy marriage? What is so unbearable for Heathcliff is the thought that he will have to stay alive when she is dead, but with his *soul in the grave*. This is the key to Heathcliff's emotional state throughout the rest of the novel. He is tortured by loss and cannot live a complete life without Catherine.

Nelly seems cool and distant from all this emotion, so much so, that when Catherine faints, she thinks *far better that she*

*should be dead, than lingering a burden and a misery-maker
to all about her.* ✪What do you think about Nelly's reactions?

There are numerous references to death in this chapter,
from Catherine's appearance, to the mention of graves. It
is clear that she welcomes death. Hell and devils and things
infernal are also mentioned. Heathcliff is always described in
these terms anyway, and their relationship is so wild and
passionate it would be difficult to associate it with heaven.

Catherine always sits beside the open window. She likes
to look across to the moors. It is as if her soul, as well as
her body, wants freedom now, and the mention of windows
emphasises this.

CHAPTER *16*

pages 201–5/146–9

- ◆ 19–20 March 1784: Catherine dies, Cathy is born at midnight
- ◆ Edgar left without a male heir
- ◆ Nelly breaks the news to Heathcliff; he curses Catherine for
  leaving him
- ◆ Catherine buried in the churchyard on the moor

The contrast between Edgar's grief and Heathcliff is typical of
them. Edgar is still and quiet and looks as if he himself has
died, whereas Heathcliff has been wounding himself against
the tree in his violent sorrow. He is once again compared to an
animal when he howls *like a savage beast.*

Cathy's birth is overshadowed by Catherine's death. Nelly also
looks at the baby and remembers that Edgar's father passed on
the property to Isabella, not Edgar. She is worried about
Heathcliff inheriting the family fortunes through his wife.

Heathcliff makes sure it is his lock of hair joined with
Catherine's in the locket. He throws Edgar's lock away, as if her
husband has no right to be connected to her.

The author uses repetition or echo again. Cathy's entry
into life is as contradictory and sorrowful as Hareton's. In
each case, the joy of a new baby is linked with the death
of the mother. Heathcliff is soaked with dew. It is as if
nature is also crying for the death of Catherine.

CHAPTER 17

pages 206–23/150–64

◆ 25 March 1784: Isabella runs away, arrives at the Grange
◆ She tells Nelly about her terrible life with Heathcliff
◆ Violence at the Heights brought to crisis point by Catherine's death
◆ Hindley locks out Heathcliff
◆ Hindley's plan to kill Heathcliff backfires, and he is shot and stabbed with his own weapon
◆ Heathcliff attacks the unconscious Hindley, but stops and binds his wounds
◆ Isabella tells Hindley of the attack the next day
◆ She provokes Heathcliff into violence towards her, then escapes
◆ She moves to the south and bears a son
◆ Edgar's depression lifts and he forms a strong bond with little Cathy
◆ September 1784: Hindley dies; Nelly suspicious
◆ Heathcliff inherits the Heights, Hareton robbed of inheritance

This chapter contains further scenes of violence. Even Isabella's choice of words shows how she has been affected. She calls Heathcliff an *incarnate goblin* and describes her attempts to exasperate him as *pulling out the nerves with red hot pincers.*

Isabella seems half mad when she arrives at the Grange and doesn't care that the house is in mourning for Catherine. She destroys her wedding ring, then describes the incredible events she has seen. Hindley is driven to kill Heathcliff but, instead, is almost murdered himself. Heathcliff's violent nature is emphasised when Isabella describes his sharp teeth.

Isabella has been so hardened by her experiences that she feels no sympathy for Heathcliff's grief over Catherine. Indeed, she hardly seems surprised to see Hareton hanging a litter of puppies. No one escapes the poison of brutality in this household, even a young child.

Heathcliff hears that Isabella has given birth to their child and makes it clear that he will take *it* when the time suits him. ❂Why does he refer to his son as 'it'?

Despite these terrible events, there is new life and hope at the Grange because of the baby, Cathy. There is contrast between her upbringing and the way Heathcliff promises to bring up Hareton. *We'll see if one tree won't grow as crooked as another, with the same wind to twist it!* ❂Who are the two trees? What does Heathcliff mean to do?

Brontë does not always describe a pleasant view of childhood. This chapter shows how children's happiness depends on the adults who raise them. Heathcliff was damaged by his upbringing and is now doing worse to Hareton. Even the newborn Cathy is described as a *moaning doll*, and is unwanted at first.

Isabella reads because she is bored and unhappy, not from real choice.

The weather is used as a background to the sorrow of the household at the Grange. Although the weather was fair for Catherine's funeral, the household is now in mourning and there is an atmosphere of sad emptiness. *The larks were silent, the young leaves ... smitten and blackened.*

Life at Wuthering Heights goes from bad to worse. Heathcliff degrades both Hindley and Hareton. Isabella escapes from her brutal marriage and describes the horrors she has seen there. Heathcliff and Catherine meet for the last time. Catherine dies, Cathy is born.

Section 5 Chapters 18–20

CHAPTER 18
pages 224–33/164–72

- 1797: 12 happy years pass
- Cathy, 13 years old, is sheltered by her father
- Edgar leaves to visit the dying Isabella
- Cathy runs off one day, ends up at the Heights
- Contrast between her and Hareton
- Hareton now a young man – no manners or social skills

This chapter adds to the sense of fairy tale that runs through the novel. Cathy is like a young princess who can no longer be protected from the bad spell (Heathcliff). Edgar tries to shield his daughter from the outside world, but it is easy to predict that she will eventually break loose. Her need for freedom reminds the reader of her mother, Catherine, and fits with the novel's idea of life being a cycle or wheel. It does not just repeat itself, however. ❂Do you think Cathy will have a better chance of happiness than her mother? What parts of the chapter suggest this to you?

We also see the effects of upbringing once again. Hareton is born into the same class as Cathy but she is brought up as a young lady, whereas he is described as *good things lost amid a wilderness of weeds.* Joseph adds to Hareton's degradation by encouraging the boy's bad manners and behaviour. ❂Remind yourself of Heathcliff as a young boy and compare the descriptions of him with those of Hareton.

Brontë uses the image of a field or garden to describe Hareton's character and his potential. *Evidence of a wealthy soil that might yield luxuriant crops.*

Cathy refuses to believe that Hareton is her cousin because he is uneducated, poorly dressed, and speaks with a local accent. Instead, she treats him like a servant.

Cathy is now at the age where she cannot be protected from the world and wants more freedom.

Mother and daughter

? Look back at your character notes or Mind Map on Catherine. Now begin adding details about Cathy. Try to build up a picture of their similarities and differences.

Cathy gets a new playmate, just like her mother before her — but Linton isn't a chip off the old block! Find out why after your break

CHAPTER 19

pages 234–8/172–6

◆ June 1797: Isabella dies
◆ Young Linton to arrive, Cathy delighted
◆ Linton is sickly and weak
◆ Joseph arrives to bring the boy to Heathcliff

Cathy is excited at the thought of a playmate, but when Linton arrives it is clear that he is weak and tearful, unlike his healthy cousin Hareton. He is made to sound very young beside Cathy, even though there is only six months' age difference.

Joseph enjoys doing Heathcliff's nasty work for him. We get a sense of children's lack of rights at this time. Linton is treated like another piece of Heathcliff's property.

CHAPTER 20

pages 239–44/176–81

◆ Linton moved to the Heights early the next day
◆ Heathcliff gives his son a harsh welcome
◆ Heathcliff reassures Nelly that Linton will be looked after properly, as he wants the boy's money

Linton is unwilling to go to the Heights, so Nelly reassures him that *all children love their parents.* ❂Why is this **ironic**?

Linton does not get a good impression of future life at the Heights, as the outside of the house looks unwelcoming and uncared for. Heathcliff makes fun of the child's pale and sickly looks. More importantly, he explains his plan of revenge. *I want the triumph of seeing **my** descendant fairly lord of their estates; my child hiring their children, to till their father's lands for wages.* He means to take the lands from the Lintons and Earnshaws, then make their descendants work for Linton and his descendants.

The idea of repetition or a cycle occurs again, in the description of Linton, who resembles Isabella and the fair-haired Linton family.

The new generation is growing up. Cathy is happy and well adjusted, Hareton is uneducated and degraded, Linton is attractive, but weak and in ill-health.

Section 6 Chapters 21–28

CHAPTER 21

pages 245–61/181–95

- ◆ Cathy distressed about Linton's departure
- ◆ Zillah speaks to Nelly about Linton's poor health and selfish ways
- ◆ Three years pass: March 1800; Cathy's 16th birthday
- ◆ She and Nelly meet Heathcliff on moors; he persuades them to visit the Heights
- ◆ Heathcliff tells Nelly that he wants Linton and Cathy to be married
- ◆ Heathcliff alters truth about the quarrel between himself and Linton
- ◆ Cathy and Linton plan future visits
- ◆ Contrast between Hareton and Linton
- ◆ Cathy makes fun of Hareton because he cannot read
- ◆ Edgar persuades her of Heathcliff's bad nature, but she is torn about breaking her promise to Linton
- ◆ Nelly finds a pile of letters from Linton to Cathy; forbids her to write again

The links between the generations continue with this chapter. The three young people meet now they have grown. Brontë sets this chapter on Cathy's 16th birthday, which is also the anniversary of her mother's death. This is significant, because her relationship with Linton begins; this marks the end of one period in her life and the beginning of another. Nelly hints at trouble to come. She describes the perfect day, then adds *it's a pity she could not be content*. When Cathy runs ahead, Nelly cannot keep up, which is a sign that the young woman is beginning to break free from the control of her father and nurse.

Heathcliff wants Linton to marry Cathy. Because old Mr Linton passed everything to Isabella and not Edgar, young Linton is the heir. ❂What is Heathcliff trying to do here? How will this marriage help him to get further revenge on the two families?

Although Heathcliff has deliberately degraded Hareton, he would have preferred Hareton for his son. Hareton is strong, handsome and straightforward. Ironically, he adores Heathcliff, even though his life has been ruined by him.

Like her mother and Edgar before her, Cathy is attracted to the fair, slender Linton, yet the pair are strikingly different. ❍Why does Cathy go along with Linton when he mocks Hareton for his ignorance?

Heathcliff can barely hide his contempt for Linton, and calls him *it* again. We also see how Heathcliff has shaped Hareton. ❍Who is Hareton compared to? Why is Heathcliff's enjoyment in ruining Hareton so very cruel? (pp. 252–3/188 *I've pleasure in him.*) Young Linton's weakness of health and character make him very different from his father. He seems to have inherited the worst qualities of young Isabella and Edgar. Zillah gives a description of Linton's selfish behaviour and later, his mockery of Hareton. Brontë is preparing us for Linton's betrayal of Cathy later in the story.

Cathy learns about Heathcliff's cruelty when Edgar tells her about Isabella's disastrous marriage. Cathy has been sheltered from the world and the story shocks her. Although she understands why she should stay away from Heathcliff, she feels great conflict about not seeing Linton. Her kind side is revealed when Nelly finds her crying about having to disappoint Linton and break her promise. It is this which makes her disobey her father and write to the boy. ❍Do you think Cathy is as wilful as her mother? What is different about the two characters?

 The gap between Hareton, and Linton and Cathy is shown mainly by Hareton's inability to read. They humiliate him for this and also for his broad Yorkshire accent.

Linton prefers to be indoors and in bed to being outside with nature. Beds are often described in a similar way to coffins or graves in the novel, so this shows how close the boy is to death.

✒ STYLE AND LANGUAGE

Windows and doors are used to show the difference between Cathy and Linton. He always prefers staying indoors to going outside, unlike Cathy who loves the freedom of the moors. He insists on having the windows closed, while she looks at the door with *longing*.

One is gold put to the use of paving-stones; and the other is tin polished to ape a service of silver. Heathcliff is talking about Linton and Hareton here. ❍Which description fits which boy? What do the two metaphors mean?

The generation game

? Look at the descriptions of Cathy and Linton. Compare these with your Mind Maps on Catherine and Edgar.

? Make a Mind Map showing similarities and differences.

? Make keyword notes about their characters as well as physical appearance.

will Heathcliff get his evil way? Find out about a budding romance after the break

CHAPTER 22
pages 262–8/195–200

♦ Edgar is ill, Cathy depressed
♦ While out walking, they meet Heathcliff
♦ He tells Cathy off for disappointing Linton, says the boy is ill with misery
♦ Cathy is determined to see Linton

Cathy feels depressed because she cannot see Linton. She is also sad because her father is ill. She expresses her fears about being left all alone. Nelly comforts her but also gives her a stern warning about disobeying her father, saying that this will put his health at risk.

We see the young woman's determination and growing maturity when she says that she must visit Linton, to make sure that Heathcliff is lying. She realises that she cannot trust

Heathcliff or just accept what Nelly says and must make up her own mind.

❂How does the weather act as a background to Cathy's mood in this chapter?

CHAPTER 23
pages 269–76/201–7

- ◆ Cathy and Nelly arrive at the Heights
- ◆ Linton ill, neglected and bad tempered
- ◆ Cathy and Linton discuss marriage, then quarrel about their families
- ◆ She pushes his chair in anger, he has a bad coughing fit
- ◆ They make it up, she mothers him
- ◆ Nelly furious that Cathy intends to visit again
- ◆ Nelly ill, Cathy looks after her and Edgar
- ◆ Cathy secretly visits the Heights at night

Joseph is his usual unpleasant self and neglecting Linton, who is very unwell. Although Nelly is irritated by the boy's miserable and complaining nature, it is clear that he is genuinely ill. He uses his illness to get attention, but is genuinely unloved and uncared for. ❂Cathy is more sympathetic than Nelly towards Linton. Whose side are you on, and why?

The hatred between Heathcliff and the Lintons is brought into the open when Cathy and Linton argue about their parents' relationships. In this way, it can be seen how the acts of the previous generation affect the children, even though they were not even born when the tragedies took place.

Cathy can be hot tempered like her mother, but she also has a kind heart, as when she does her best to calm Linton. She does not bear grudges, whereas Linton milks the situation for as long as he can. Their relationship is more like brother and sister or mother and child than of future man and wife.

Nelly tries to put Cathy off Linton by telling her that he will not live long. ❂Do you think she is wise to do this? Why?

Cathy shows her growing independence in two ways. Firstly, she declares *The Grange is not my prisoner, Ellen, and you are not my jailer.* Then she visits the Heights, despite being forbidden to do so. Cathy now has to take more responsibility for the family by looking after Nelly and her father, but she is also determined to have more life for herself.

Real love

? Find examples of the way Linton treats Cathy as a mother figure. Underline the quotations and annotate your copy of the novel if you are allowed to, or write it up in your Mind Maps or notes.

Hareton tries to better himself, but is mocked. Linton and Cathy fall out. Find out how — after the break

CHAPTER 24
pages 277–87/207–16

- ◆ 1800: Nelly discovers that Cathy has been visiting the Heights
- ◆ Cathy becomes the narrator
- ◆ She tells Nelly about her visits
- ◆ Cathy and Linton's idea of a perfect day
- ◆ Hareton has taught himself to read, but Cathy makes fun of him
- ◆ He is angry and throws Linton and Cathy out of the kitchen
- ◆ Linton is very angry and has a coughing fit
- ◆ He blames Cathy for the incident when she returns
- ◆ She forgives him and they make it up; she learns to accept his behaviour
- ◆ November 1800: the narration returns to Nelly, who tells Edgar everything; he stops the visits

The shift between Nelly and Cathy as narrators in the last two chapters shows us another side to Linton. Brontë lets Cathy speak, and we see her describing her relationship with the boy from her point of view. It is also a sign that the young woman is making her own decisions, rightly or wrongly.

Cathy makes fun of Hareton's attempts to educate himself. This is thoughtless and cruel. He wants her approval and is so angry when she throws it back in his face, that he throws Cathy and Linton out of the kitchen. ❂What do you think Hareton feels about their relationship?

Linton's rage at this is like a weak version of Heathcliff's, and typically, Joseph enjoys seeing the boy angry and powerless. It is also typical of Linton that he rejects Cathy, the one person who really cares about him. It is only Cathy's affection and concern that makes her return and make up their quarrel. Linton shows a rare moment of honesty when he apologises. He loves her and dislikes himself, but cannot improve his behaviour. Cathy is realistic about his nature, but very loyal to him, because she realises he has no one else.

STYLE AND LANGUAGE

Cathy has persevered with the visits to Linton, even though he has often behaved badly to her. The quarrel they have about heaven tells the reader a lot about them. Cathy's heaven is full of wind, light and movement, *the whole world awake and wild with joy.* Linton just wants to lie still all day in the sun. It is rather like his desire to stay in bed and not take part in life, whereas Cathy's heaven shows her energy and enjoyment of all living things.

Linton and Cathy share a love of books. Hareton wants to be included into this world so tries to teach himself to read. Cathy also uses them to bribe a servant so she can visit the Heights.

CHAPTER 25
pages 288–91/216–9

- ◆ 1802: the narration returns to Nelly
- ◆ She teases Lockwood about his fascination over Cathy, then returns to story
- ◆ Summer 1801: Edgar close to death, confides in Nelly about his fears for Cathy Linton writes a letter asking to meet Edgar; Nelly suspects some of it written by Heathcliff

◆ Edgar agrees to let the pair meet on the moors
◆ No one realises how ill Linton is

Nelly teases Lockwood about his interest in Cathy but he refuses to do anything about the young woman. ❶How does this remind you of Lockwood's actions in the first chapters of the novel?

Edgar is dying, and worries about Cathy being left alone when he is gone. He does not care about Heathcliff getting his own way, but is concerned that Linton will be too weak to protect Cathy from Heathcliff's *wickedness*. After Linton's letters and Cathy's pleading, he allows them to meet on the moors. No one realises that the boy is dying and that Heathcliff is *avaricious* (greedy) and *unfeeling* by forcing him to ride and walk with Cathy. Nelly does not realise this until later, of course, so her comments are made in hindsight (knowledge obtained after the event).

Edgar always visits his wife's grave on Cathy's birthday, but this time he does not. It seems as if he is so close to death that he knows he will be reunited with her soon. Linton is also dying.

Brontë's use of two dying characters, as well as the pattern of very short chapters at this point of the novel, adds to the sense of events moving quickly.

CHAPTER 26
pages 292–6/219–22

◆ August 1801: Nelly accompanies Cathy to meet Linton
◆ He looks ill and weak, but calms Cathy's fears, although Nelly alarmed
◆ He seems frightened of his father

Linton is very changed, and Cathy cannot understand it, although Nelly fears the worst. She is direct and asks him if Heathcliff has started beating him.

Cathy is naive about Linton's ill-health, just as she does not understand that Edgar is dying. She is disappointed in Linton, who is too ill to respond to her, but begins to worry about him on the way home.

Ironically, the 'heavenly' summer's day once described by Linton as perfect, is here, but he is too ill to enjoy it.

CHAPTER 27
pages 297–309/223–33

- ◆ August 1801: Edgar fading fast, hopes Cathy will be happy when she is married to Linton
- ◆ Cathy and Nelly meet with Linton again
- ◆ He is weaker than ever, paralysed by fear
- ◆ Cathy unsympathetic at first
- ◆ Heathcliff arrives and threatens the boy
- ◆ Cathy forced to go to the Heights to protect Linton
- ◆ Heathcliff locks them in
- ◆ Cathy stands up to him, but he beats her
- ◆ Heathcliff plans to force them to marry
- ◆ Nelly locked up for days on her own

The beautiful August weather seems to give hope and life, yet is tinged with sadness because Edgar is dying. It also provides a strong contrast with Heathcliff's cruelty and violence. Linton's fear is so strong and Nelly is so puzzled by it that it seems almost supernatural. Linton is *powerless* against it.

Cathy's behaviour towards Heathcliff lets the reader see why she became the angry, bitter person that Lockwood met at the beginning of the novel. Despite her courage, he beats her. Heathcliff is made even more angry by the resemblance to her mother.

Nelly does not understand Cathy's willingness to marry Linton. ❂Why does Cathy want to marry Linton? Is it just so she can be with her dying father?

 ## STYLE AND LANGUAGE

The language in this chapter becomes more urgent and desperate, as Linton tries to avoid Heathcliff's violence, Nelly and Cathy try to escape from the Heights and Heathcliff makes sure the pair are married before Linton dies.

Heathcliff keeps the two women prisoner, and has also threatened to lock his sick son out of his home. Cathy is physically and emotionally trapped by the situation because her father is near death. The windows are too narrow to let them escape. Cathy's mood matches the changing light on the moors.

Wordpower

? Make a list of as many words or phrases in this chapter which describe fear or anger. For example, distraught, trembled, snatched, struck, curbed ferocity.

*dire deeds and death. Find out about
Heathcliff's villainy after the break*

CHAPTER 28
pages 310–16/233–8

- ◆ Nelly released by Zillah the housekeeper
- ◆ Linton will not help her to release Cathy
- ◆ Nelly returns to the Grange
- ◆ Edgar intends to alter his will so that Heathcliff cannot inherit when Linton dies
- ◆ September 1801: Cathy escapes, is with her father when he dies
- ◆ Heathcliff has bribed the lawyer, so Edgar cannot change the will

Nelly reminds Linton about Cathy's kindness to him. His conscience is not stirred, all he is interested in is her money. The word 'marriage' is never mentioned, but he speaks of owning everything that once belonged to Cathy so it is clear that the wedding has taken place. This is an echo of his father's own loveless marriage to Isabella.

❂Why does Heathcliff destroy the portrait of Edgar from Catherine's locket? Who was in the other portrait? The separation of the two portraits is a symbol – of what?

Cathy escapes through her mother's bedroom window by the fir tree, and her return to the Grange is marked by a soft, persistent knocking. These details are another example of the novel's circular form, because they are a reminder of her mother's ghost trying to get into Lockwood's window at the beginning of the novel.

Three years pass. The new generation meet again. Secret letters and visits between Cathy and Linton. Hareton and Cathy clash, as do Linton and Hareton. Echoes of the generation before them. Linton very ill, Edgar also. Heathcliff kidnaps Cathy, forces her into marriage. Linton gets the family money and Edgar dies without being able to change his will in Cathy's favour - the next step of Heathcliff's revenge is achieved.

Section 7 Chapters 29–34

CHAPTER 29

pages 317–22/239–43

- ◆ September 1801: Thrushcross Grange now Heathcliff's; he walks in to claim it
- ◆ Linton has been punished, is mad with fear of Heathcliff
- ◆ Cathy forced to go the Heights and care for him
- ◆ Heathcliff describes Linton's vicious nature
- ◆ Cathy still loves Linton, expresses her pity for Heathcliff
- ◆ Heathcliff tells Nelly about looking at Catherine in her coffin
- ◆ He has had coffins changed so that he can lie next to her

◆ When Catherine was first buried, he tried to dig up her body, but felt her spirit near him and was comforted
◆ Since then, she has come and gone; he has lived in torture
◆ He takes Cathy back to the Heights; Nelly forbidden to visit

Edgar has only just been buried when Heathcliff comes to claim his inheritance. Heathcliff is pitiless, as can be seen by the way he enjoys Linton's fear of him. Cathy's pity for the lonely, miserable Heathcliff, is spoken in *dreary triumph*. Already, the loveless atmosphere of the Heights is affecting her.

Heathcliff's macabre description about looking at Catherine in the grave shocks the reader and makes us realise just how obsessed Heathcliff is about being reunited with his love. There are hints that he will be a wandering ghost if he is not buried next to Catherine. ✪Why does he speak of *sleep* rather than death?

We learn that this is not the first time he has tried to get at the buried Catherine, as he tried to dig her up when she first died. He describes the past 18 years as torture. Catherine has been as unpredictable in death as she was in life, sometimes visiting him in spirit form, but leaving him alone most of the time. ✪What are your feelings towards Heathcliff at this point?

Death and sleep are described in almost similar ways. Perhaps this is a sign that Heathcliff sees death as a welcome rest from his unhappy life. It also suggests that he believes in some sort of after-life with Catherine. Graves and beds are described in a similar way. For example, when Heathcliff tries to sleep in Catherine's old room, her spirit stays with him, even lying on the pillow. The reader does not have to believe in ghosts. What is important is that Heathcliff is convinced of Catherine's presence, and has been affected by this belief for half of his life.

CHAPTER 30

pages 323–9/243–8

◆ Zillah gives Nelly news; Cathy is unhappy and disliked by everyone

- Linton is ill, Heathcliff refuses to get the doctor; Zillah will not help Cathy
- October 1801: Linton dies, Cathy all alone and penniless She stays upstairs for two weeks
- Comes downstairs one Sunday, rejects Zillah's and Hareton's help
- She allows Hareton to fetch books for her
- He strokes her hair, she is angry with him
- Cathy cuts herself off from anyone's help, grows more bitter and bad tempered
- January 1802: Nelly finishes her narration, Lockwood announces that he is leaving for London

Linton dies, with only Cathy to mourn him. She also feels *like death*, and locks herself away. Her return to the household is like returning to life, even if it is miserable and unwelcoming. She cannot bear to stay in the freezing upstairs room, but the cold is also emotional. It is as if her unhappiness has frozen her spirit. She says she has been *starved,* a Yorkshire term for cold, but this is a reminder of her mother's refusal to eat at the beginning of her illness. ❂There is a similarity between the way mother and daughter react to extreme unhappiness. Can you see a difference between them also?

Another reminder about the circular style of the novel is the way uncouth Hareton is so similar to young Heathcliff. Both are embarrassed by the presence of a beautiful and educated young woman and tried to clean themselves up. Cathy is proud like her mother.

It is significant that when Cathy returns to the household and gets warm, she immediately turns to books. Perhaps this is a sign that she is taking some pleasure in life again. Hareton helps her to reach the books, and wants her to read to him. Although she rejects him, he is beginning to share in the world of books.

CHAPTER 31

pages 330–5/249–53

- Lockwood takes Nelly's message to the Heights
- Cathy rejects the letter, Hareton lets her have it back

- Heathcliff has destroyed her books
- Hareton embarrassed when Cathy says she has found his hidden books
- He gives them to her, despite her rudeness
- She continues to humiliate him about his poor reading skills
- He throws the books into the fire, even though he does not want to lose them
- Lockwood guesses Hareton's reasons for wanting to read
- Heathcliff returns; he looks *restless* and *anxious*
- Lockwood invited for dinner

Lockwood is uncomfortable at the quarrelling between Hareton and Cathy. Cathy has grown more spiteful because of her unhappiness. Lockwood realises that Hareton wants to be accepted by Cathy, which is why he is trying to read. She is angry at the way he reads her favourite books so badly and continues to provoke him. He burns the books, even though they have brought him so much pleasure.

Heathcliff comments on the growing resemblance between Cathy and Hareton. ✪What has happened to Hareton to make the resemblance more obvious? We also get an idea that Heathcliff feels affection towards Hareton, for he mutters *it will be odd, if I thwart myself.* Heathcliff worries that he will spoil his revenge by helping Hareton.

Books are Cathy's link with a better, happier life, which is why Heathcliff destroys them. Hareton wants to be part of this because he is attracted to her. He also gets pleasure from words and ideas, because his natural intelligence has been starved for so long.

CHAPTER 32

pages 336–46/253–63

- September 1802: Lockwood is back in the neighbourhood
- Nelly no longer housekeeper at the Grange
- Lockwood visits the Heights
- The place is welcoming and homely
- Sees Hareton and Cathy reading together
- Nelly singing, Joseph complaining

- ◆ She returns to her narration
- ◆ January 1802: Nelly returns to the Heights to care for Cathy
- ◆ Easter 1802: the beginnings of friendship between Cathy and Hareton

Wuthering Heights is changed, and so is the behaviour of its inhabitants. Things are so different that Lockwood describes Hareton and Cathy without mentioning their names. ✪What is the effect of this on the reader, do you think?

Another important sign of change is in the behaviour of Nelly and Joseph. He is still twisted and speaks of Hareton being 'witched' by Cathy, but he has lost his power to hurt now. Nelly sings happily and just laughs at him. She is also warm and welcoming towards Lockwood.

Nelly brings Lockwood up to date. When she returns to the Heights in January, Cathy has become more bitter and quarrelsome, but there are important signs of change when she tries to heal the divisions between herself and Hareton. Cathy is a little like a princess in a fairy tale here, because her kiss transforms him. *He trembled and his face glowed – all his rudeness, and all his surly harshness had deserted him.*

The window and door symbolism is used here to show the change in Cathy's life. At the beginning of the chapter, the windows and doors are open, but when it moves back in time, Cathy is still a prisoner, sitting by the window but unable to go outside.

Cathy gives Hareton the present of a book and puts his name on the parcel. It is a sign that she now wants to welcome him into the world of books - and take him as a friend.

Same house, different lives

?   Can you see the difference in the appearance of the house on p. 338/255, compared to its description on pp. 46/20 and 51/23–4?

?   How do the changes in the house fit in with the changes in the lives of the characters?

? Make a Mini Mind Map to show the contrasts, using key words.

who dug up the currant bushes? Take a break before finding out

CHAPTER 33

pages 347–55/263–70

◆ March 1802: Cathy and Hareton move Joseph's currant bushes to make a flower bed
◆ Heathcliff tells Cathy off
◆ She accuses him of having stolen wealth from herself and Hareton
◆ Heathcliff threatens to throw out Hareton if she carries on influencing him
◆ Hareton refuses to believe anything bad about Heathcliff
◆ Heathcliff notices the resemblance of Cathy and Hareton to Catherine
◆ He describes his feelings about the two young people
◆ He has lost the urge for revenge, and also his will to live

The removal of Joseph's fruit bushes is a sign that change is coming to Wuthering Heights. The young lovers want to change the prickly bushes for a beautiful bed of flowers. This is a sign that they are taking control of their home, and also that the harshness of Heathcliff's and Joseph's rule is coming to an end. Another example of the change is Cathy's playfulness when she puts primroses in Hareton's porridge. Heathcliff cannot stand their happiness. She also confronts Heathcliff about the inheritance for the first time.

Heathcliff's anger with Cathy is frightening, but his mood changes and he looks at her intently. ●Why do you think he changes his mind about hitting her?

Hareton is loyal to Heathcliff. ●Do you think he is right? How does Hareton's behaviour show the difference between the two generations?

Heathcliff's conversation with Nelly shows that the past is catching up with him. He is haunted by Catherine. Not only do Cathy and Hareton remind him of her, but everything does. *The entire world is a dreadful collection of memoranda that she did exist, and that I have lost her!* He longs for death.

CHAPTER 34
pages 356-67/270-9

◆ April 1802: Heathcliff avoids everyone
◆ He returns one day, his behaviour is *wild and glad*
◆ He stops eating
◆ Nelly is frightened by his appearance one evening
◆ She dreams about him
◆ He continues to refuse food. He sees things that no-one else can see
◆ Nelly tries to persuade him to see a minister – he is not interested in Christian ideas of heaven
◆ May 1802: goes to his room and refuses to come out; Nelly finds him dead
◆ Hareton grieves for him
◆ Local people say Heathcliff's ghost walks
◆ Lockwood leaves, avoiding the young lovers
◆ Visits the three graves, does not believe in the ghost stories

It is spring at the Heights, time of new life and hope. Hareton and Cathy work on the garden, a symbol of their new life together. Heathcliff, on the other hand, avoids company and stops eating, a sign that he is ending his life. His behaviour becomes unpredictable and strange, but he is not violent or angry. The way his happiness is described makes him seem unnatural and frightening.

Everything associated with Heathcliff's illness and death is described in a supernatural way. Look also at pp. 359-60/272-3 (*The light flashed on his features ... left me in darkness*). ❸Why does Nelly think such things? Do you think she is just superstitious?

This theme is continued when Heathcliff sees things invisible to others. In death, his face has a *life-like gaze of exultation* (triumph, joy). ❂What do you think he saw as he died? Although Nelly says she does not believe in the local tales about the ghosts of Heathcliff and Catherine, she does mention her meeting with the frightened young shepherd who has seen something. Only Lockwood is sceptical (unbelieving). However, he runs off from Hareton and Cathy to avoid seeing them, just as he did in Chapter 32. He brings his loneliness on himself, but cannot bear to see the happiness of others. He won't believe that the dead lovers are restless in their graves. ❂Do you think he is the sort of man who understands such a powerful love? What is your opinion about whether the souls of Heathcliff and Catherine rest in peace or not?

Heathcliff inherits all. Linton dies and Cathy falls into despair. The relationship between Hareton and Cathy develops. Heathcliff loses the will to live and dies. Love and decency return to Wuthering Heights in the form of Cathy and Hareton's impending marriage.

now you've finished going through the text, take a well-earned break

TOPICS FOR DISCUSSION AND BRAINSTORMING

One of the best ways to revise is with one or more friends. Even if you're with someone who hardly knows the text you're studying, you'll find that having to explain things to your friend will help you to organise your own thoughts and memorise key points. If you're with someone who has studied the text, you'll find that the things you can't remember are different from the things your friend can't remember – so you'll be able to help each other.

Discussion will also help you to develop interesting new ideas that perhaps neither of you would have had alone. Use a **brainstorming** approach to tackle any of the topics listed below. Allow yourself to share whatever ideas come into your head – however silly they seem. This will get you thinking creatively.

Whether alone or with a friend, use Mind Mapping (see p. v) to help you brainstorm and organise your ideas. If with a friend, use a large sheet of paper and thick coloured pens.

Any of the topics overleaf could feature in an exam paper, but even if you think you've found one in your actual exam, be sure to answer the precise question given.

TOPICS

1 Discuss the idea of love and marriage in the novel. Make a Mind Map of the characters who marry. Decide on the good and bad points of each marriage.

2 Heathcliff is a monster and the reader cannot feel any sympathy for him. Discuss this idea, then MOG! (**M**ind Map, **O**rganise, **G**ather)

3 Why does Emily Brontë use flashback in the novel? Look particularly at the last four or five chapters.

4 What's in a name? Do a brainstorm for each name in the story. For example, how does Heathcliff's name fit with what you know about his character?

5 Make a Mind Map about the theme of 'books' in the novel. Show the ways in which books are used by different characters for good and bad purposes. For example, Edgar Linton reads to escape from the problems in his relationship with Catherine (bad), whereas Hareton reads because his mind has been starved of ideas and beautiful things (good).

6 Write a short character study comparing Catherine and Cathy.

7 With a friend, role-play Heathcliff being interviewed by a local newspaper reporter after Linton's death. Get your partner to ask you questions about how you got hold of your money. Imagine the angry replies Heathcliff would make!

How to get an 'A' in English Literature

In all your study, in coursework, and in exams, be aware of the following:

- **Characterisation** – the characters and how we know about them (e.g. what they say and do, how the author describes them), their relationships, and how these develop.
- **Plot and structure** – what happens and how it is organised into parts or episodes.
- **Setting and atmosphere** – the changing scene and how it reflects the story (e.g. a rugged landscape and storm reflecting a character's emotional difficulties). This is called 'pathetic fallacy'.
- **Viewpoint** – how the story is told (e.g. through an imaginary narrator, or in the third person or through a series of different narrators).
- **Social and historical context** – influences on the author (see 'Background' in this guide).

Develop your ability to:

- Relate **detail** to **broader content, meaning and style**.
- Show understanding of the author's **intentions, technique and meaning** (brief and appropriate comparisons with other works by the same author will gain marks).
- Give **personal response and interpretation**, backed up by **examples** and short **quotations**.
- **Evaluate** the author's achievement (how far does the author succeed and why?).

Make sure you:

- know how to use paragraphs correctly
- use a wide range of vocabulary and sentence structure
- use <u>short</u>, appropriate quotations as 'evidence' of your understanding of that part of the text – don't just stick large chunks down for the sake of it!

- answer the question, don't just tell the story. Your teacher and the examiner know it already – you've got to show that you can apply your understanding to one particular part of the novel, such as a theme or a character.
- use literary terms to show your understanding of what the author is trying to achieve with language. Some hints are given below as to what examiners will consider 'good' and 'bad' answers.

Good – Brontë compares Heathcliff to *bleak hilly coal country*. This metaphor emphasises the dark, ugly side of Heathcliff's character.

Bad – Brontë uses lots of interesting metaphors.

Good – *The larks were silent* at the beginning of Chapter 17 suggests that even the birds are miserable after Catherine's death. Brontë uses pathetic fallacy in this example to convey the sorrow and loneliness felt by Nelly and Edgar.

Bad – Brontë uses lots of descriptions from nature. These give atmosphere. (This is bad because there isn't an 'example' from the story. Even if you can't remember the correct literary term, you will get marks for giving an example to explain what you mean).

THE EXAM ESSAY

You will probably have about an hour for one essay. It is worth spending about 10 minutes planning it. An excellent way to do this is in the three stages below.

1 **Mind Map** your ideas, without worrying about their order yet.
2 **Order** the relevant ideas (the ones that really relate to the question) by numbering them in the order in which you will write the essay.
3 **Gather** your evidence and short quotes.

You could remember this as the **MOG** technique.

Then write the essay, allowing five minutes at the end for checking relevance, and spelling, grammar and punctuation. **Stick to the question**, and always **back up** your points with evidence in the form of examples and short quotations. Note: you can use '. . .' for unimportant words missed out in a question.

Model answer and essay plan

The next (and final) chapter consists of a model answer to an exam question on *Wuthering Heights*, together with the Mind Map and essay plan used to write it. Don't be put off if you think you couldn't write an essay to this standard yet. This is a top 'A' grade essay – a standard at which to aim. You'll develop your skills if you work at them. Even if you're reading this the night before the exam, you can easily memorise the MOG technique in order to do your personal best.

The model answer and essay plan are good examples for you to follow, but don't try to learn them off by heart. It's better to pay close attention to the wording of the question you choose to answer in the exam, and allow Mind Mapping to help you think creatively.

Before reading the answer, you might like to do a plan of your own, then compare it with the example. The numbered points, with comments at the end, show why it's a good answer.

MODEL ANSWER AND ESSAY PLAN

QUESTION

How does Brontë create an appropriate atmosphere and background to the events of *Wuthering Heights*?

PLAN SUMMARY

1   First impressions – Chapter 1
2   Moors
3   Weather and <u>storm</u>
4   Two houses
    a) Wuthering Heights
    b) Thrushcross Grange
5   Conclusion – link this to final chapter

ESSAY

'Wuthering Heights' contains scenes of great drama and emotion, and Brontë gives the reader a feeling of this right from the beginning of the novel. In Chapter 1, we get important clues about the inhabitants in the way she describes the 'stunted firs' and 'gaunt thorns'.[1] These are harsh images and resemble the miserable people inside.[2] Hareton is stunted because he has not been educated or brought up properly, Catherine is unhappy because she has lost everyone and Joseph is a bitter, twisted old man. The author then mentions the 'narrow windows' and makes the house sound like a fortress to keep others out. This introduces the atmosphere of suspicion towards strangers which continues through the novel.[3]

Brontë also uses the moors as a background[4] to what is happening to the characters. For example, Lockwood is puzzled by the relationships between Heathcliff, Cathy and Hareton, just as the reader is. The snow storm that traps him at the Heights in Chapter 3 adds to the feeling of confusion because it changes the appearance of everything on the moors,

and he gets lost.[5] Later on, Catherine and Heathcliff run wild out of doors, to escape the cruelty and neglect of Hindley and Joseph. The moors become linked with the two children, especially Heathcliff, because he is an elemental character.[6] This means that he is ruled by natural or primitive forces, just like the moors themselves, which can be full of energy and beauty or wild and cruel. Catherine and Heathcliff love the moors because they are like themselves.

The weather is another important way of creating mood. One rather sad example[7] is after Catherine's death. Although it is spring, the weather is wet and cold, and 'the larks were silent, the young leaves of the early trees smitten and blackened'. Brontë describes the day as if it is also in mourning for Catherine. The words 'blackened' and 'smitten' are dark and depressing, making it seem as if the leaves have also died.[8]

There is a huge storm on the night that Heathcliff leaves the Heights, which Brontë describes very dramatically. 'The growling thunder ... the storm came rattling over the Heights in full fury ... there was a violent wind'. The use of personification[9] is vivid and makes the storm sound angry at what has happened. This fits in with the idea that Heathcliff and Catherine are one. A split between them is so unnatural that it goes against nature, and even the weather seems to protest.

The atmosphere of the two houses is another[10] important way of telling the reader about events and characters. After Hindley has turned to drink and Nelly has left, Wuthering Heights changes from a place that is warm and homely to being neglected and dirty. Even though there is often trouble and argument at the Heights at the beginning of the story, we still read about warm fires and meals being cooked. There is a sense of ordinary human life going on amongst the unhappiness. Later, Isabella's letter to Nelly describes great changes. There is still a fire, but no other light, and the floor is 'grey' with dirt, and the pewter dishes have lost their shine. I think Brontë is suggesting that there is darkness inside the characters, not just in the house.[11]

However, the greatest difference is seen in Heathcliff's bedroom. The curtains and bedding are all ripped and there are dents in the walls, as if he has kicked or punched them.

This is a powerful example of the way that Heathcliff's violence and destructiveness affects everything around him.

Thrushcross Grange is also described in different ways. In Chapter 6, it is 'a splendid place carpeted with crimson'. Heathcliff finds it beautiful, but it is also too 'soft', rather like the spoiled young Lintons who live there.[12] It is the first time Catherine has experienced such luxury, and this is the beginning of the divisions between herself and Heathcliff. Later in the story, Heathcliff returns and Catherine has to face up to the terrible conflict in her life. The Grange and all it stands for is not enough. The strain gives her a breakdown and she dies.

In the final chapter of the story, Brontë shows the reader that love and order have won at Wuthering Heights. She creates an atmosphere of peace and harmony by describing the 'sweet and warm' spring day and the gardening done by Hareton for Catherine – a symbol of growth and new beginnings for the living.[13]

WHAT'S SO GOOD ABOUT IT?

1 Use of a short quotation as part of a sentence.
2 Discusses the quotation and gives own suggestion as to its meaning.
3 Shows how one example fits in with an idea or theme from the whole novel.
4 Understanding of how the setting affects characters.
5 Gives a specific example of this.
6 Shows how background can be a symbol for an important character.
7 Personal response about the example given.
8 Original interpretation of the author's words. Gives an opinion about Brontë's choice of words.
9 Use of a literary term to explain how the author achieves an effect.
10 Another example of how atmosphere is created, with evidence from the story.
11 Understanding of what the author is doing in this example.
12 Shows similarity between place and people who live there.
13 A final example about atmosphere and background which brings the essay to a neat conclusion.

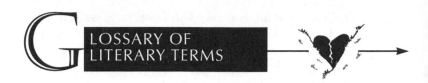

GLOSSARY OF LITERARY TERMS

accent a combination of how people pronounce words (e.g. Joseph's *frough morn tuh neeght*), which Emily Brontë suggests by spelling, and their intonation (ups and downs in the pitch of their voices).

alliteration repetition of a sound at the beginning of words; e.g. ladies' lips.

context the social and historical influences on the author.

dialect local words used in speech (e.g. Joseph's *hearken* for 'hear').

foreshadowing an indirect warning of things to come, often through **imagery**.

image a word picture used to make an idea come alive; e.g. a **metaphor, simile,** or **personification** (see separate entries).

imagery the kind of word picture used to make an idea come alive.

irony (1) where the author or a character says the opposite of what they really think, or pretends ignorance of the true facts, usually for the sake of humour or ridicule; (2) where events turn out in what seems a particularly inappropriate way, as if mocking human effort.

metaphor a description of a thing as if it were something essentially different but also in some way similar; e.g. *her eyes radiant with cloudless pleasure* (Ch. 21).

pathetic fallacy similar to **personification**, it gives human feelings and emotions to nature; for example, the *growling thunder* in chapter 9 makes the storm seem angry about Heathcliff's departure from Wuthering Heights.

personification a description of something (e.g. fate) as if it were a person.

prose language in which, unlike verse, there is no set number of syllables in a line, and no rhyming.

rhetorical question one asked for effect or as a figure of speech, expecting no answer; e.g. Heathcliff, *How the devil is he so like?* Ch. 31).

setting the place in which the action occurs, usually affecting the atmosphere; e.g. the moor.

simile a comparison of two things which are different in most ways but similar in one important way; e.g. Heathcliff speaking of Linton: *I'll crush his ribs in like a rotten hazelnut* (Ch. 11).

structure how the plot is organised.

theme an idea explored by an author; e.g. death.

viewpoint how the story is told; e.g. through action, or in discussion between minor characters.

INDEX